T0129420

EFT

CONSTELLATIONS

Heart-Centred Processes for Self-Confidence & Healthy Independence

MARY LLEWELLYN

BALBOA.
PRESS
A DIVISION OF HAY HOUSE

Copyright © 2018 Mary Llewellyn.

EFT Founding Master, BA(Hons) F.R.S.A.

All rights reserved. No part of this book may be used or reproduced by any means, graphic, electronic, or mechanical, including photocopying, recording, taping or by any information storage retrieval system without the written permission of the author except in the case of brief quotations embodied in critical articles and reviews.

Balboa Press books may be ordered through booksellers or by contacting:

Balboa Press
A Division of Hay House
1663 Liberty Drive
Bloomington, IN 47403
www.balboapress.com
1 (877) 407-4847

Because of the dynamic nature of the Internet, any web addresses or links contained in this book may have changed since publication and may no longer be valid. The views expressed in this work are solely those of the author and do not necessarily reflect the views of the publisher, and the publisher hereby disclaims any responsibility for them.

The author of this book does not dispense medical advice or prescribe the use of any technique as a form of treatment for physical, emotional, or medical problems without the advice of a physician, either directly or indirectly. The intent of the author is only to offer information of a general nature to help you in your quest for emotional and spiritual well-being. In the event you use any of the information in this book for yourself, which is your constitutional right, the author and the publisher assume no responsibility for your actions.

Any people depicted in stock imagery provided by Thinkstock are models, and such images are being used for illustrative purposes only. Certain stock imagery © Thinkstock.

Print information available on the last page.

ISBN: 978-1-5043-9728-5 (sc)
ISBN: 978-1-5043-9729-2 (hc)
ISBN: 978-1-5043-9730-8 (e)

Library of Congress Control Number: 2018901551

Balboa Press rev. date: 02/24/2018

Praise for EFT Constellations

As a person, it is only normal to question our lives, and wonder whether it's normal to question our own existence and purpose; do other people do it too? It's refreshing to read that you're not the only one to question life, to want to go against the dogmatic path set out for you, no matter how hard that's going to be.

Mary shares her story, and bravely tells how she herself went against the grain of life, even though it was possible she could be outcast. What doesn't break you makes you, and that it did for Mary.

Within these pages you'll learn new ways to manage and deal with life. Mary's style of writing will really connect with you, and you'll energetically feel her compassionate warmth come through the words. Mary openly shares her wisdom and vast knowledge in the field of alternative therapy. Many of Mary's clients have stated that by using some of the techniques and resources, which you'll learn about in this book, was akin to hitting the emotional factory re-set button, allowing them to move on in life, without the social conditioning and past hardships that have led to low self-worth.

EFT Constellations will open your eye to the real magic of energy medicine. Mary takes us on a journey to meet some of the pioneers in this field, who have developed the modalities which will help you connect with your true self. When you can be your true authentic self, that is when you come alive and are able to show up in the world as nature intended.

I am very grateful to Mary for writing this book and putting these much-needed resources – which sometimes are deemed esoteric and not of any worth – out in to the world in a way we can all understand and benefit from. This work is important, because it gives hope to those who may have tried other therapies, to no avail, but energy therapy offers new hope, not just to people, but to the world as a collective whole. The world is changing, and the way we take care of ourselves needs to change with the world. People do not realise just how powerful they are, and that they can heal themselves. This book will teach you how you can heal yourself, if you take you power back.

- By James Gardner, author of *How To Heal From Trauma And PTSD: Your ultimate guide to becoming the person you want to be,* and life coach at Live Your Greatness. www.liveyourgreatness. life

I first met Mary over 12 years ago now. I had suffered with an eating disorder for 10 years, which was sparked by a childhood trauma. It was after receiving hospital treatment that I was directed to Mary for therapy.

After I had medical treatment for my condition I knew I wanted to get better but I felt that I would never be able to be free of my anorexic habits. They had taken root in my mind and it was the only way of life I knew.

Instantly Mary spoke words to me that made me feel that I could do something about this. I was sceptical about EFT at first. I had always been interested in yoga and meditation, but I had never practiced practical methods like tapping or journal writing.

My therapy with Mary followed the methods in the book. Using a journal allowed me to become in control of my thoughts, as I began to understand how the inner chatter in my head worked. And it allowed me to start to balance the negative voices with positive, pro-active ones. The EFT worked as a physical act of taking back control. By saying something out loud and with purpose I could retrain myself to be strong minded. I was no longer victimised by my own thoughts, or sabotaged by my past.

The success of Mary methods is in the sustainability of it. Deciding to make a change is only the first step. Living with the changes can be very challenging. Mary's methods bring you back to reality so you can be yourself and not someone affected by a negative, self-destructive state. Judging yourself gives you permission to feel low and defeated. Mary showed me a way out of all that, into a state of mind where I now feel happy and calm.

I will always continue to stay in touch with Mary. She was a guiding light in dark times and her ways continue to resonate within me.

- Kay Leggott

"What a wonderful read EFT Constellations is. From the word go, I was hooked and felt as if the author was writing to me personally. Understanding the writers own journey makes you feel less alone in knowing that no matter how challenging your personal situation you can turn it around using the insightful questioning and range of self-help techniques included within.

This book is a heart centred guide to making informed choices and becoming more connected with who you are. The content rich chapters offer you the opportunity to gain more self-acceptance and healthy independence as well as increased confidence and an understanding of self. This ultimately leads you to a place of calm and serenity enabling you to enjoy and appreciate life more.

This empowering read explores how mind and body connect and provides simple, practical and effective strategies to remove blocks, treat pain, aid sleep, improve relaxation and guides you towards enjoying a sense of achieving more balance, harmony and purpose in your life. A must read for anyone who feels stuck and who wants to move forwards in life"

- Wendy Fry Author of Find YOU, Find LOVE and Mothers and Daughters

I've known Mary Llewellyn and her work for over a decade. Back in the days when I was also contributing to the field of EFT, Mary and I were on the same circuit and our paths crossed many times. What always struck me about Mary's work was that it contains a lot of heart. She shows up as a unique individual who lives by her truth and deeply cares for every person who crosses her path. It's with that same spirit and intention that she has written this book. It's no surprise to me that her opening sentence is, "As you read this now, are you looking for opportunities to follow your heart?" because that, in essence is what Mary does with her work. It's a book that I would recommend to anyone who wants to amplify their journey with EFT. It's a unique opportunity to connect with a heart centered EFT master who is caring and committed and who genuinely wants the very best for you. Whether you are a practitioner looking to deepen your experience, a client who wants to understand more about the process of EFT, or someone who is practicing EFT on their own and wants to deepen their journey, this book will give you unique perspectives that you can integrate into your own practice, or your practice with others.

- Sasha Allenby, co-author of Matrix Reimprinting Using EFT, author of Write an Evolutionary Self-Help Book.

Mary Llewellyn (Mair) has gone through tremendous challenges in her own life, being raised in a restrictive religious sect, which I would label as a cult. We share this in common, and in order to leave such a situation, it requires great inner and outer strength to start over again, especially with children in your care. In order to enter society, there is a great amount of healing that needs to take place. I am so impressed with Mair's focus on helping herself heal, so that in return, she can help others heal, all in the comforts of our own home! EFT Constellations is a loving gift from a loving woman, to assist all of us in heart-centered processes for self-confidence and for healthy independence of our traumas and reactions. In other words, regardless of what has happened to us in the past, we can regain our true selves through the many healing modules that are described in this phenomenal book. Thank you, Mair!" ~ Wendy Sue Noah, Author of "Real Eyes Faith"

- Wendy Sue

Contents

Foreword

I have had the pleasure and honour of knowing Mary Llewellyn for over fifteen years. Mary was one of my first teachers in EFT, and she is someone whose passion and knowledge for energy psychology lit my own path and fuelled my enthusiasm to explore these amazing, life changing techniques.

Mary was one of the first EFT Therapists in Europe, having trained in 1999 with the AMT. She was at that time a Director of that organisation. She continued her journey with Energy Therapy and became one of the first EFT Founding Masters in 2005. She is one of a very few to be given this title by Gary Craig, the creator of EFT. She remains a firm friend of Gary's and visits him at his home in California.

Her interest in Energy Therapy led her to investigate various forms of this therapy such as Tapas Fleming's TAT and Larry Nims's BSFF. She has trained in a number of Energy Therapies and has become a trainer in many of them.

She continues to study these therapies and practices them in her clinic at Tickhill, South Yorkshire, UK. As well as treating clients with a wide variety of problems, she teaches practitioners at all levels and runs an active Mentoring Group.

Her book does not intend to be a training text in any of these therapies, although it contains an outline of the methods employed by many of them, as it is assumed that readers will already be familiar with at least some of the therapies covered. Readers who do not have this familiarity will gain a sufficient insight into the various therapies to enable them to decide if they should seek a formal training in any of them.

The book is intended to pass on the experience that Mary has gained during her long involvement in practicing and teaching these therapies, as well as in her life generally. In this she succeeds very well. I hope this book will be helpful to readers at all levels.

Karl Dawson
EFT Founding Master
Creator of Matrix Reimprinting
Hay House Author
2016

Introduction

EFT CONSTELLATIONS – Heart-Centred Processes for Self-Confidence and Healthy Independence

As you read this now, are you looking for opportunities to follow your heart?

Do you sense, deep down inside yourself that you have so much to give and to share with others?

Are there days in your life when you instinctively see exactly what you want to achieve?

And on another day, do you plunge into self-doubt and ask yourself, how am I ever going to be free of my fears?

Are there times when you feel a lift and then moments later, your inner chatter throws cold water on your good intentions?

Could these experiences be connected to the steps you intend to take towards healthy independence and more freedom?

A little of my own story

All the questions I have asked you so far were similar to the ones I asked myself, day in day out, as I was growing up. As time went by, I experienced a growing drive to get out of the restrictive religious sect I had been brought up in. I was in my mid-twenties and happily married to a man who was also a member of this sect. Each day it became clearer to me that my husband, our three young daughters and

I deserved freedom from the limitations that had been imposed upon us throughout our lives.

Life with my birth family was very insular; my loving parents believed that their restricted way of living was the one and only path for them and their six children. As time passed me by, it seemed to be an impossible dream to separate from this life and my family. Even though I knew exactly what I needed to do and why, I had no idea of the how.

On some days, I could see a way to leave. Then moments later, my confidence drained away, and I felt sad, anxious and powerless. This conflict went on and on, until one day something changed. I knew instinctively that leaving the Exclusive Brethren and my family was very important. And having experienced so many restrictions throughout life, I really didn't want our lovely daughters to grow up with massive limitations too. Fortunately, my husband felt exactly the same about the life we were living as I did. We also knew that our own health and happiness as parents were essential for us all.

I wished it could be different; however, I felt deep inside that the only real course of action open to us was complete separation. When I was little, three of my older brothers left home. No one explained to me why my brothers left, or where they were. I began to think it was because they felt the same way that I had begun to feel. When my husband, our children and I finally left the sect, it was an unbelievable wrench. I was leaving my lovely mum, dad, sister and brother and I knew it was unlikely that we would ever see them again – for I knew that as soon as we left, we would not be allowed any more contact.

After leaving, it was a relief – it was clear how the controlling restrictions this sect had consistently imposed upon all of our lives had deeply infected the whole of our family. Now that we were free, we could make our own decisions. Experiencing freedom and the ability to make informed choices in life seemed strange at first.

Our children could now have contact with and make friends with other children. Life took on new meaning: there were so many openings. A short while later, when our local doctor confirmed that I was pregnant with our fourth baby, we were overjoyed. I immediately joined a group of other pregnant women and learnt about a book called *The New Childbirth* by Erna Wright.

This book taught me how to use a deeply relaxing method intended for childbirth. This baby's birth experience was totally different from my three previous daughters' births. I discovered shortly afterwards that this was self-hypnosis. The birth had been a life-changing experience: it spurred me onto learning and training in hypnosis. I really wanted to share with others just how versatile self-hypnosis could be for many aspects of life. In 1980, when our youngest daughter started school, I opened my private hypnotherapy practice. I continued my studies at the same time and gained an Honours degree in Psychology and a postgraduate advanced diploma in Child Development Training. Since then I have received training in a number of Energy Psychology therapies in the USA with all of the developers.

Since 1999, my husband and I have been training practitioners and trainers in the UK in EFT. Then, in early 2000 our training expanded into many countries and this included teaching EFT, BSFF, TAT and self-hypnosis for birth for doctors. (Later on in the book I will talk about these different modalities.)

Also, after intensive EFT training, we both became EFT Founding Master practitioners under Gary Craig in 2005. I continue to love and enjoy my calling and it is an honour to share my experiences with students and clients, and to teach and work with my mentoring groups. To this day, I absolutely love it when, after working with clients, they ring to say they are now free to get on with, and really enjoy, their lives.

What about you and your story?

Are you asking yourself questions about your life as I did about mine?

I wonder, are there experiences from your early life or in your life today that still hold you back or stop you in your tracks?

When you notice a state of flow with experiences of genuine happiness, do you ask yourself how or why this is happening?

Then, on other days have you felt blocked or intimidated by chatter in your head or by destructive comments made by someone else? When this happens, does your inner conversation whisper, "I will never, ever, be able to do what I really want to do."

Have you realized that you have been, and are, consistently exposed to other people's criticism? Does this come from what you are thinking or is it from the situation that you find yourself in?

PART ONE – EXPLORING: Getting to Know You

Here are ways this book will help you

Chapter One - Finding Yourself in Your Journal

Chapter Two - Reflecting and Writing in Your Journal

As you continue to read, I introduce steps for you to take so you can enjoy more balance and purpose in your life. One of the most important is journal writing. The strategies that I share with clients and students are included in this book and can be incorporated into your personal journal writing as you continue to explore getting to know you.

The benefits of journal writing for clients came to me early on in my private hypnotherapy practice, and all the feedback from my clients confirms that journal writing is invaluable. They say it keeps them moving forward and on track.

Also, clients have found that their journal thoughts help enormously towards their personal self-hypnosis practice.

As I saw how and why journaling worked well, I streamlined the process: clients now find they need fewer appointments – and this has always been my intention. I love sharing techniques that offer healthy independence.

Chapter Three - Link Hypnosis to Your Journal Intentions

Fairly early on in my hypnotherapy practice, I realized that a client's own personal links to words, sounds, images, feelings, tastes and aromas were keys to their neurology. I became very aware of how naturally clients connected to their unique associations; these then became their most valued assets. In fact, the ways in which we represent how we think and feel need to be combined whilst using hypnosis. If words, images, sounds and feelings and so on do not resonate inside us, then they will have little or no effect. The same rule applies to you when you are helping yourself.

There are examples in Chapter Three of how to link self-hypnosis to your own journal intentions. You will be encouraged to explore your earlier resourceful times and will be given ways to implement them during your self-hypnosis practice. I've also provided descriptions of the valuable nuggets that others have discovered and successfully incorporated in their lives. As you read how other people have utilized their previously forgotten areas of confidence, calm or freedom, you'll see why this is so valuable.

Chapter Four - The Bridge Technique

The combining of hypnosis and EFT seemed to happen more or less by accident. When I was using EFT with clients, I realized that they were often in a trance-like state. And in that state, they were more able to access early experiences including both negative and positive memories. Clearing their distress or trauma with EFT allowed them the benefit of reconnecting to their early positive and resourceful states. These were the springboards that launched them towards their personal growth as well as healthy independence.

The Bridge Technique and other tools I share with you in this chapter have the capacity to reconnect you to who you were born to be, and it is why this book's message is uniquely able to serve you. The gifts that were given to you at your conception are still there to be activated again. They may have been submerged or wrapped up, and now you can welcome them with love again. Some students and clients have called this their re-alignment process. Others have described it as their factory reset button and say that they feel it brings with it wonderful experiences as well as a sense of being complete, or whole. One client explained, "It's like I've been reborn with all of my lessons and learning intact."

(More detailed information and case histories of The Bridge Technique can be found in the chapter entitled *Creating a Bridge to our History* in the Appendix.)

PART TWO – DISCOVERING: Finding and Accepting You

Chapter Five - The Miracle of Mind and Body Connection

This chapter is about finding and accepting you and noticing how your thoughts can affect your physiology. It offers you more information of how stress and tension affect the rhythm of your heart, your breathing, digestion, sleep and immunity. This takes you towards discovering more about you and how your mind and body function together.

Your subconscious mind retains early experiences that may have created anxiety inside you at a specific point in time. These events are often forgotten consciously, however they can still automatically trigger a stress response even though this may not be relevant now. I found that learning more about the science behind the mind and body gave me practical ways to help myself and others if triggering occurred. I hope that you may find this is useful for you too.

The next three chapters describe three different energy therapies

Energy therapies offer wonderful ways to remove blocks. They free up the flow of energy, which benefits health in our body and brain. Each chapter presents a different energy therapy. The developers use their therapies in unique ways – they can add other dimensions to your life and your work.

Chapter Six - Emotional Freedom Techniques (EFT)

Gary Craig was keen to expand his own personal development and that of his clients in his financial advice services business. He trained in Thought Field Therapy (TFT) with Dr Roger Callahan in the 1990s, and afterwards, he created EFT. He saw the amazing benefits of this energy therapy, and teaching EFT to others became, and still is, his passionate calling.

A way to describe EFT simply is that it helps with emotional as well as physical pain. Gary says it is like emotional acupuncture – and doesn't use needles. The way in which this clears the disruption in our body's energy system is remarkable. It is a simple self-help technique that can be used by anyone. When I first heard about this, I knew it would be one of the most effective and empowering techniques I could give to those I met. In this chapter I share how EFT can be of enormous help to you.

Chapter Seven - Tapas Acupressure Technique (TAT)

Tapas Fleming was an acupuncturist who helped clients with their environmental allergies. Later in her work she followed her intuitive guidance and created TAT. These changes meant that she no longer needed to use needles.

Tapas offers her clients a simple and practical way for them to gently touch points on their face with one hand and at the same time, use their other hand to support the back of their head. When in this position, you allow your mind to wander around your problem. There is no therapist intervention: just guidance through a number of steps. The positive results of this energy therapy technique help you when you are feeling emotional and when you experience physical discomfort. In this chapter, you will learn how to use this on yourself.

Chapter Eight - Be Set Free Fast (BSFF)

Dr Larry Nims is a psychologist who, like Gary Craig, did his energy therapy training in TFT with Dr Roger Callahan. Following the training, he decided to simplify what he had learnt; consequently he developed his own technique, BSFF. For a few years he used a smaller number of tapping points which clients found helpful. A number of years later, Larry found that clients were getting better with an even simpler technique that he still uses today.

PART THREE – CELEBRATING: Loving Care for You

Chapter Nine - Energy Therapy Gifts for Your Life

This chapter introduces you to an interesting selection of deceptively simple ways to help yourself and others. They include novel ways to use EFT or other therapies in a way that may not be familiar to you. In some circumstances, just touching one acupoint may easily remedy a problem. I will also be introducing gentle ways to help with tension, pain or for relaxing at night. You can use these self-help tools even when other people are around.

A list of the major therapies you will meet:

SET (Simple Energy Therapy) – Steve Wells and David Lake
TAB (Touch and Breathe) – John Diepold
Energy Medicine – Donna Eden
The Choices Method – Dr Patricia Carrington
TFT (Thought Field Therapy) – Dr Roger Callahan

Chapter Ten - Loving Confidence and Independence

This chapter concentrates on confidence, healthy independence and interdependence. Many of us may have developed low self-confidence from an early or later experience. This can happen if we have been judged, bullied at school or received critical parenting at home or belittling treatment or comments in the workplace. Distress is not only felt in early life: it can happen to any of us, especially when we experience loss. This may be loss of a relationship, a loved one, loss of financial security or of changes to one of our physical faculties. All or any of these can give a jolt to our system.

I have frequently noticed that we can be critical of ourselves for the way that we feel or react. Judging yourself can become so natural and it can be very painful. This chapter is intended to support and encourage you by building healthy independence and confidence in a compassionate and understanding way.

Chapter Eleven - Heart-Centred Nourishment for You

This chapter encourages us to see the tremendous value of showing compassion towards ourselves and each other. When forgiveness and respect are shared, this care flows to us all. In most circumstances we are, and often have been, doing the best we can in view of our own history. Self-acceptance and kindness add trust in what we do, as well as in the way that we intend to give.

This chapter illustrates additional strategies that can support your life and help you towards a deeper understanding of your desires and towards a more expansive and meaningful life. You will be able to explore your abilities that were perhaps not as visible to you before. When you know that you deserve to be cherished and nourished, making time and the intention to include times for this will create surprising shifts in yourself, as well as in the way you relate to those you love and the people you have contact with. The title of this chapter suggests coming to this moment with the intention of being your very own best friend. When you cherish yourself and show compassion and forgiveness for your mistakes, trust is felt inside. And as you support and encourage others, you can sense more quickly when they need a little tender loving care. The heart-centred processes you will read about are simple choices to offer you care as well as ways to care for those around you.

Chapter Twelve - Meditative Choices Bring Peace to You

Enjoying more peace with mind has added many benefits to my life. Those I work with have been surprised at how much this has nurtured them too. I have assembled a number of ways to gain more calm and serenity in your life. A large part of what is written here for you was gathered from my own journey. Clients and students have also had a huge input. They have been wonderful teachers to me. Each one generously gave me gifts: neither of us were aware of it at the time, but later on, after times of reflection, I saw this clearly. As you read this now, know that I dream of you becoming more connected to who you really are as a result of our journey together. I also wish that your positive energy will flow through you and out to those you love and to other lives that you touch.

Now that you have read this introduction to your chapters, you have a little taste of what is to come. I look forward to our journey through this book. I hope the book gets very dog-eared as it continues to support and inspire you. With blessings from me to you.

PART ONE

EXPLORING:
Getting to Know You

CHAPTER ONE

Finding Yourself in Your Journal

Find your voice and passion to activate your dreams
Be present, appreciate life and experience your blessings
Understanding, trusting, supporting and loving yourself whatever
happens
Be consistently true to yourself

Reconnect to who you really are in your uniqueness

Welcome to Chapter One. Its intention is to connect you to material that will add to the talents and abilities that already belong to you. Whilst reading this, more of who you really are will begin to emerge. The structure of what we do together will light your way towards even clearer purpose. This is your time for considering and finding out more of where your real desires lie.

I'll be providing you with ways to really listen to yourself, and as you actively listen to your thoughts, you are open, and this creates time for your needs to surface. Then you can register that you wish for more purpose or you can voice your needs and express exactly where your confidence could do with a lift. We frequently gloss over these areas that connect us to our vulnerability. Expressing how you would like to react in life opens up and identifies your own unique possibilities that can take you towards creating your desired responses.

Jotting down your fleeting thoughts in a notebook will help you to retain your insights. I learnt that I couldn't always trust my memory. Once, I completely forgot a title I was pleased with. It was intended for a blog I had already written. Now, and a long time later, that title continues to elude me. So now, I write my insights down.

Also, when I forget to jot down my thoughts, I am disappointed because sometimes there may have been a hidden gem. Don't make the same mistake as I did and miss a light bulb flash of inspiration coming to you. Research suggests that physically writing down our thoughts not only helps our recall – it actually begins the process of moving us towards something we are wanting to achieve.

So… please find a notebook you can carry easily in your pocket. That way it will be handy and helpful for the recall of ideas as and when they come to mind. Sometimes they appear out of thin air – a quote, a colleague's comment or an interview you happen to overhear. Collect these in your pocket notebook to keep and we will work with them in more detail in the next chapter.

Also, be on the lookout for a really beautiful or quirky journal that you would love – it will belong to you, exclusively. When you get it, keep it safe for now. Later, you will just love to write in it. You may itch to start in it, and soon you will do as you read Chapter Two.

Here are the personal areas you will be exploring in your journal when you arrive at Chapter Two. There are three sections that you will find useful to write in your journal.

What are your desires in life?	The front of your journal
What are you truly grateful for?	The centre of your journal
What do you really want to let go of?	The back of your journal

The Front Pages in your journal – for your passionate desires

When you write down what you want to bring into your life in the front of your journal, you will have a place where you can develop, expand and generate your dreams. Writing down your desires and being fully connected to your heartfelt intentions frequently stimulate energetic opportunities for you in your life.

Find your voice and passion to activate your dreams

The reticular activating system (RAS) is a part of your brain that subconsciously searches for what you are intentionally consciously wanting. This is why when you see, hear or intuitively sense what you have consciously dreamed of, this part of your brain alerts your awareness to this. However, if your desired intentions have not been registered specifically on your perceptual radar, they will continue to be outside of your awareness. As you write in your journal, something incredible is happening for you: these intentions are automatically connecting through all of your senses to this wonderful part of your brain.

The Centre Pages of your journal – where you acknowledge gratitude and appreciation
Be present and appreciate life and experience your blessings

This section is where you enjoy time for reflecting on what touches your heart and soul. When you write here, you can appreciate being at peace in the here and now.

Paying attention and making connections to whatever makes your heart sing will bring even more smiles to your life.

The Back Pages of your journal – when writing here, you really listen and learn to respect and honour your own needs

The back of your journal is where you will be welcoming yourself with kindness and knowing that you are experiencing an honest and intense desire to be loving to yourself. How often have you been really attentive to others – your family, friends as well as work colleagues – and not given the same to yourself?

This part of your journal is your time for you to be totally available for you – to genuinely listen, understand, notice and respect your own unmet needs.

More previews for Chapter Two

What you can write in your journal's three sections

In the front pages of your journal, you'll be writing what you are genuinely wanting, or asking yourself how you would prefer to react in a current enjoyable or challenging situation.

In the centre pages of your journal, you will have the opportunity to record simple heart-warming happenings: to notice someone's friendly smile, a kind word or your really comfy shoes. If you wish to, why not start a gratitude list in your pocket notebook whilst in this chapter. These may be simple uplifting moments which feel good. This can become your beautiful daily practice in your journal.

Understanding, trusting, supporting and loving yourself whatever happens

The back pages of your journal will be where you write for just a few moments early each day. This ensures that you become more tuned into you and to what is going on. When you care for and pay attention to yourself, you can more easily notice sad, confused or difficult experiences. In these early morning moments, you are listening, seeing, feeling and being your very own best friend.

The thoughts and feelings that you notice are all evidence that you need to love and take care of yourself. So, even a reticence to start to use your beautiful book in Chapter Two is offering you a message to take better care of yourself. Will you make a way so that you can do this for you? I believe that when we treat ourselves kindly it not only helps our health and happiness – it can also spread love to those around us. We regularly eat and drink without thinking it is odd. As you begin, and continue, to write, so can your journal nourish you with physical, emotional and spiritually good experiences as well as bring joy into your life.

It works exceptionally well if what you write in your journal is a stretch for you as well as a practical possibility. Even if you have no way of knowing how a particular dream can actually happen, that questioning which comes from your logical conscious mind is so normal. Right now, in your pocket notebook, write something that gives you an excited instinctive experience inside. It's ok if what you write seems entirely imagined. Sometimes goals and dreams can start from a tiny seed that was planted when we were really young.

Someone once told me that when she was little, an aunt gave her a book containing paper clothes and a cardboard dress up doll. Interestingly enough, now she is a successful fashion designer! What you write may be something that comes from your childhood or something that seems to come out of thin air! Your writing in your journal is a process of growing and exploring yourself. And when you allow yourself to be open, you are naturally creative.

In the 1970s I had a dream and this dream was to help other people. I started on this path by studying psychology. When my GP asked me why I was studying psychology, I said, "I want to teach people to be more positive." He laughed when I said this, but I knew that was what I wanted to do – even though I really didn't know quite how I was going to get there! I did do what I wanted to do, even though sometimes my inner conversation resisted change and I was afraid. I know this is normal for everyone. Sometimes we can worry about people's image of us, or a whole host of other reasons. Our YES BUTs which come up are all part of the way we question ourselves. You too will hear your YES BUTs and I hope you will write them down when you get started in your journal because this will help you too.

Absolutely everything we do is related to a thought, or comes about by ideas, words, images and feelings.

"Thoughts are the fuel that ignites the spark of creativity within us."
Mary Llewellyn

For example, scientists needed to think about a possible visit to Mars for this to actually happen. Large as well as small things come into being in this way. For instance, thinking of something really useful meant someone created the deceptively simple 'post it' notes. Much of what surrounds us was once an idea inside somebody's head. That's how dreams and visions are born – they are thoughts, gut feelings, desires, images and possible solutions to problems together with our positive intentions – solutions to problems – which have all been connected with our desire for wish fulfilment. Our own personal writing manifests thoughts that feel instinctively true to us.

Be consistently true to yourself

The wording of what you write in the front part of your journal is a bit like an affirmation, or a statement of intent. If this really resonates with your intention, it can be applied to novel areas of your life. However, the most important part of this is what these specific words mean or feel like to you. Words, images, feelings, sounds, tastes and aromas have unique associations for you. They are keys to your neurology. These associative links are already registered within your mind and body. Much of this book is about joining these up, so that you can link your dreams to your already existing skills and resources. Writing down with a positive intention begins the process. If something comes to you here, why not put it in your pocket notebook ready to recall for your journal later.

Numerous skills are accessible to you, and writing in the front of your journal provides connecting keys to inspirational resources that already belong to you. They could have come from an exciting event that happened yesterday or even from an experience one or two years ago. Right now, are you thinking that you have no connecting link into the area that you wish to develop? Is your desired objective a completely unknown quantity to you? Have you felt feelings that you are really wanting now in another scenario? If you have these thoughts, the aim now is to focus on the feeling, image or a time whenever you enjoyed a state of flowing with what you were achieving. When you've done that, whilst you are connected to that positive feeling or image experience, maybe taken from another time, just guess at how good that state of mind and body would feel in your imagined future time or place. If you wonder how this could possibly happen that's very normal – just think that and let it go. Then write brief notes in your pocket notebook to remind you of what came to you. These are ready then to write out in more detail when you begin your journal. If an uplifting statement comes to you now, do put that in your notebook in readiness too. This then gives clarity to your focus, as well as a blueprint to your mind. When you do this, it guides your mind towards a clear and specific end result that you are wanting. When we are specific and passionate, our desires awaken our RAS. Then, as mentioned above, this part of our brain will alert us whilst we move in the right direction. Each time we register our sense of knowing that we are actually on track, it strengthens as well as deepens our trust in the process.

Reconnect to who you really are in your uniqueness
How to intentionally access a positive inspirational resource to use now or for the future

How a client connected to a positive resource

This is a simple example of how a client accessed a positive resourceful state. Even though this positive experience happened when she was a little girl, her reconnection took effect in her life again and helped her. This client came for help because she was sleeping through the sound of her alarm clock in the morning. This meant that she was arriving late for work. Not surprisingly, her late arrival resulted in her receiving a verbal warning.

The worry about losing her job was the reason why she came to see me. When I asked her what she would like to do instead of sleep through the sound of her alarm, she seemed lost for words about how she wanted to react when the alarm went off. Her thoughts of losing her job had frozen her with fear. As she couldn't think of anything, I asked her if she would like to feel refreshed when the alarm went off. The expression on her face told me she didn't like my suggestion at all!

Apparently, her personal association to the word 'refreshed' had really negative connotations for her. In her mind, this word was connected to the UK's Heineken beer advertisement and she hated it. The word that I suggested would not have helped her at all. At the end of her first appointment, she left with the intention of finding a word, image or experience that would help her to wake when her alarm went off.

(It is crucially important for you to use your own words, images, sensations and memories to inspire yourself personally. Any association that gives you good feelings will work well for you.)

When this client returned for her next appointment, she proudly gave me a piece of paper with her own intentions that were taken from the front of her journal.

As she handed her list to me, I could tell straight away that her energy had changed. I guessed that she had unearthed a truly powerful link to an experience. It was obvious that this would help her. The first statement on her list of wishes was: "When the alarm goes off I feel invigorated." Now, 'invigorated' is not a word I would generally use. However, I knew then that this word carried positive energy for her, so it was exactly the right word to use. I asked her what 'invigorated' meant to her, and she said, "Oh Mary, when I was a little girl I used to go riding early on a Saturday morning and as we rode into the fields, the early morning mist was rising and I felt so invigorated."

The fact that this word belonged to years ago and had no obvious relationship to her current situation does not matter.

It is the state of being which we need to capture so that we make a successful link.

Within each and every one of us, there are many resources, such as those that are in the archives of our mind as well as our body to connect to. Her childhood horse riding experience gave her just what she needed. What she personally did to help herself in finding this memorable association meant she never received a written warning!

Other options to create links to success

Did the previous paragraph make sense to you? Do you have associations of good states to connect to? If the previous paragraph did not work for you, there are other options that you may well find helpful.

In some circumstances, a positive role model is invaluable to follow. Would-be snooker players and sports enthusiasts avidly watch the winners play for this reason. Other people listen to eloquent presenters with the intention to learn more about their delivery, their timing, and watching their body language. Role models are inspirational and surprisingly they do build confidence. As you watch and study them, you may wonder how it would feel for you to experience this state of being. With practise, you guess at what it would be like to step into their shoes. Some people look at a mirror to practise or they record their performance so that they can see and hear, as well as coach, themselves. On my way to presentations I often rehearsed what I wanted to say during the drive there. No doubt other drivers thought I was strange, but fortunately I never saw them again! Other possible choices of a role model could be an older brother or sister you look up to.

Again, if this new desire or your role model was conjured up from an experience in a different setting from the intended state you wish for, that poses no problem – it will still work for you. What is important is your determination to move towards whatever it is that you are wanting. Clarity is a huge plus, when the way you imagine or the way you feel excites you. The energy of your excitement connects you to the benefits you receive in the end. Being specific about your desires for yourself personally is what is so helpful. Ask yourself, "How will it serve me, and in what ways will it benefit others?"

Notebook Reflection Point

Now, at the end of this chapter, pause a moment, take out your notebook, and jot down any insights that may have come to you as you read along. They could be to follow a dream or make a difference to your life or something else. Whatever you write down now will be important links to what we'll do in Chapter Two and beyond.

Chapter One: A Brief Summary

This chapter welcomes you to:
Get to know yourself
Discover examples of your personal desires
Choosing your own way to follow through
Writing down your desired process so you keep on track
Discover how your results will be achieved

CHAPTER TWO

Reflecting, and writing in your journal

Give yourself joyful times whilst getting to know yourself

Keeping the journal present in your developing conscious awareness opens up intuitive understanding towards who you really are. You actually notice your feelings, your tastes, the images, the sounds and the aromas surrounding you. You see that they happen all of the time – sometimes they take a back seat and at other times they may be really present.

Move through unhelpful emotions and reactions in your life

As you become aware of what your physical senses are telling you, you also become more aware of how your own inner chatter influences you. And rather than treating it as something unwanted or irritating, this inner chatter can be a window to seeing, feeling, hearing and knowing what is important or truly relevant to you. This often comes in the form of fleeting messages that we receive from inside, and being aware of these gives us a chance to question what may be only our conditioned response. These responses may relate to early childhood experiences. Perhaps they were words our parents, teachers or friends said to us. We may often treat them as truths – rather than the hearsay, or examples of another person's perception of us at a particular point in time, that they are.

What if writing in the front, middle and back of your journal is your gift of time for you to reflect on these new messages? You may see that this will flag up choices for you to consider which bring growing support and inspiration to you. Then, when you find you have genuine desires to free your mind of the unhelpful chatter, you'll find some help. These questions can bring answers to you, as you become more present and actively involved in your life.

"And every day, the world will drag you by the hand, yelling, 'This is important! You need to worry about this! And this! And this!
And each day, it's up to you to yank your hand back, put it on your heart and say, 'No. This is what's important."
Ian Thomas

Getting started in your journal

Now it is time for you to get started inside your journal. If you haven't already bought your journal yet, I recommend that you stop now, and buy your journal before continuing. Previous to my journal writing, many times I found scraps of paper notes scattered around, and then one day I realised I deserved a lovely book for me to write in. You do too, so, buy one that you would enjoy giving to someone else you love ... and then give it to yourself. Why not give your journal a name that has a lovely association for you? Or one that has a happy connection from your past? Clients and students tell me that a personally appealing book works so much better for them. Your specially chosen book will give you a warm, friendly message whenever you pick it up and write in it.

Sometimes people say to me that writing and expressing their thoughts and desires honestly in their journal is difficult or perhaps too personal a way to write. Do you think that too? Or, do you wonder, "If I start to write I may make a mistake and have to cross something out!" Or do you maybe think that your book is just too good for you to use? I had similar feelings to this when I was given a lovely leather-bound book to write my gratitude experiences in! It sat in a drawer unused for a very long while. Please use your special book! I have noticed that writing really does help to clarify our thoughts and feelings – it is a wonderful way of finding yourself.

Can you recall a moment when some gentle or kind person really took an interest in you or in what you had to say? What did you feel? What ideas came clearer to you as a result? Your journal can be your way of being there for you.

The Front of Your Journal
This part is for expressing what you are wanting

Find your voice and passion to activate your dreams

When you picked up *EFT Constellations* and bought it: why did you buy it? What were you hoping for? The front of your journal is asking you about those hopes and dreams. What are you passionate about in life now? Last thing at night, let your mind wander with positive expectancy for gifts of inspirations when you awake. What do you wish to receive that would help you to be true to yourself? Without thinking too much, ask yourself the question, "What do I value above all else? Where in my life do I enjoy exciting energy?" If something helpful comes to you when you ask yourself that question at night or here as you're reading, or when you are out and about, jot it in your pocket notebook. Later, you can write these thoughts in your personal journal.

Creating structures that support your heart's desired intentions

Creating distinct areas in the front of your personal journal will make it simpler and really accessible for you. Write down a few headings specifically related to what you are wanting for yourself. Here are some examples: Professional self-confidence, Personal healthy independence, Spiritual practices, Study focus, Harmonious relationships, Family connections, Social situations, Sports performance, ... or? Choose headings that are personally relevant and important to you and not necessarily my suggestions. Please also write about what applies to you and your needs.

Below, I've provided an example of how you could work with "Professional self-confidence" in your journal.

Professional Self-Confidence

Your practice gives you more energy to mobilize your skills. It is here that you reflect on how you want to feel and on responses you are hoping to receive from your colleagues, clients, trainers or managers. When you have given these intentions time to percolate, it is crucial to ask yourself for a similar state, feeling or place of when you effectively handled whatever is problematic for you now.

How a client's reconnection to previous areas of competence helped him again

Here, including intentions and results, is what a client, a young executive whom I'll call Hal, wrote regarding criticism at work:

Desired intention: When my manager is critical of me, I am self-confident and naturally able to reconnect to an empowering state of calm confidence which I enjoyed feeling whilst working at ……….. in 2015.

Desired result: Reflecting on my experiences of self-confidence is empowering me all over again, and I communicate calmly, respectfully, and persuasively.

Hal came to see me for help with his recent television presentations. He discussed with me how frustrated he felt to be struggling with this, as it was a complete surprise to him. He described himself as a very confident communicator and was very confused now to find that this new TV opportunity was making him freeze on the set. Finding himself lost for words was completely foreign to him.

Hal described to me how he really enjoyed leading and inspiring his team on a regular basis during their weekly meetings. He found that it was simple and comfortable for him to go with the flow: that was his natural style. The group as a whole reported a real sense of achievement during their meetings. These were his previously felt areas of competence that he reconnected to again.

Following his hypnosis sessions, he realised that he had been overwhelming himself with too many bites of information for his TV delivery. This insight allowed him to limit his presentation to two or three bullet points. His decision automatically anchored him to his natural gift of free flow during his television presentation, and this carried over to his regular professional team meetings.

Hal's journal note:

Whilst reflecting after these experiences, Hal put this note into his journal. "My journal notes help me keep it simple for my free flow."

Below, under the next group of headings, there are other examples of responses that could work for you. Why not adjust these subheading examples or create relevant headings to reflect what you are really wanting even if this is only to explore some future possibilities?

Harmonious relationships

Jennifer wrote:

Desired intention: It is just as easy and comfortable for me to be open with my nephew as it was when my brother-in-law Jim and I sorted out our own family misunderstandings last Christmas.

Desired result: Whilst we talked together, I noticed, as well as felt, my nephew warming to my genuine interest and honesty. This naturally brought us much closer together.

Jennifer's journal note:

"My journal notes often remind me of how being honest and caring enriches my relationships."

When we choose well-defined desired objectives, it enhances our clarity.

Knowing what we are wanting and holding a desired end result in mind is pivotal to the success of any venture.

Driving to any destination requires us to know just where we are heading for the success of our arrival. In just the same way as a journey, our knowing specifically what we are wanting for our life is equally important. Discovering the way we want to feel and how we intend to react is important for our future self-confidence, our happiness and growing independence.

Work-desired objectives

Wendy wrote:

Desired intention: When my manager is reviewing the report I have written, I gently and intentionally let go by breathing out. Then, when I calmly take a breath in, it is easy for me to respond skilfully and appropriately.

Desired results: After taking a calming breath, it is easier for me to really listen as well as respond to her respectfully and confidently.

My response to my manager dramatically improves our joint understanding and this benefits many other members of our team.

Wendy's journal notes:

"I found I was incredibly calm and able to really listen to my manager as she reviewed the report I wrote. I have since used this simple calming breath rhythm for many occasions. This has added to my confidence, which is also helping my professional performance."

Below are some brief, sample *Desired results* just to give you possible areas you may wish to consider in your journal. Making the content

personally specific to you will make a valuable difference to your life.

Family

Desired results: I am learning deceptively simple ways to build an even closer relationship to my dad. Times spent with our families are happy as well as surprisingly enjoyable for us all.

Friends

Desired results: My friends and I often help each other and afterwards we relax together: I enjoy thinking over those memories. Even days later they warm my heart.

Team Group Project

Desired results: When I am open and honest, it is easy for me to ask team members for their support and helpful ideas. Then afterwards we all notice how much this has benefitted our cricket pavilion project as well as the team's performance.

Leisure

Desired results: During my yoga practice I feel good, and afterwards, I enjoy experiencing calm in my mind as well as my body.

Desired results: I enjoy an energetic buzz when creating arty things with my children.

Health

Desired results: My health and energy levels improve following my morning run. After doing this for a couple of weeks, I see that it helps me to relax and drift easily off to sleep at night.

Desired results: Making time for myself and being more mindful has opened me up to love in my heart and soul.

Healthy eating and drinking

Desired results: Using my instinct in my choice of food is a loving and thoughtful way to care for myself.

Desired results: Making healthy choices when I am eating and drinking sends powerful self-worth messages to me.

The Centre of Your Journal
This part is your gratitude section

Be present, appreciate life and experience your blessings

Here are a few ideas just to get you started. Write whatever touches you with warmth, laughter and joy.

The centre pages of my journal bring me confidence, positive enthusiasm and happiness. Noticing and being thankful for wonders however small, nurtures and uplifts me.

I remember a wonderful memory with friends who are a big part of our lives. Then, I notice it still spreads warmth inside as I recall our closeness. I consistently feel their love as well as the fun we shared together.

When you write in this part of your journal, really link up to your experience of gratitude. Notice what it feels and means to you to have walks in your garden, or down a dreamy country lane and to feel the sun on your back or how good it tastes to be savouring healthy foods when stopping to share a picnic with family or friends.

Your reflections on life include genuine thankfulness and often bring warmth and colour to you again. Have you ever held the corner of a teabag in a cup of boiling water and watched its colour swirl through the water? I have frequently found that appreciative feelings colour and warm my life in the same way.

Here are just a few more:

Thank you for my work colleagues' support today.

It feels so good to be able to handle my boss's criticism more calmly.

I appreciated being asked for help by my brother.

Thank you. I loved the beautiful rainbow today.

Experiencing thankfulness, however short, changes our state of wellbeing. When you put your attention on what is enjoyable, you notice how this affects your energy levels: you then see how your intentions really change your state. And when you are in a thankful state, you embed an association (like embedding suggestions during hypnosis) so that you receive more and more of the same benefits and enjoyment. This cycle of positive energy helps to light up your life.

A client's gratitude story

This client (I'll call her Lily) told me that her husband Tom had lost his sight a number of years ago. I asked her what she was able to do to support herself and her husband at this time of their lives. She told me that each morning she walked around her local duck pond. When she did this, she sat on one of the benches and just watched, savouring this scene with all of her senses. She really opened herself up and absorbed all the images and said, "I can see." She told me that she saw all of this as if for the first time: she drank in the beauty. It was like seeing and looking and taking it in through new eyes.

Whilst she did this, she reflected on how it felt for her to be so close to nature. On her way home, she bubbled over with all of these beautiful images and feelings. When she arrived home, she shared these experiences lovingly with her husband. She said how she had felt as she looked around and gave glowing examples of what she had seen. She chose words that were very colourful and expressive and her voice was animated as she opened her heart to paint a picture for him.

And as she did this, he smiled as he saw and felt her feelings and imagined seeing through her eyes. She really valued her sight, so each day she would share stories with him. They felt as if they had actually been there together.

On a later appointment, Lily shared with me how she had written her desired intentions in the front of her journal to awaken herself to insights of imagery, light and aromas for Tom's life. Here are the words she used for her desired intention: "Each day I see creative ways to bring light, visions and magical colours into Tom's life – these, and the aromas I collect, delight his senses."

Then, a week after that appointment she thought of a unique way in which she wanted to reconnect Tom to even more openings in his life. In the front of her journal she wrote many detailed memories that she remembered of the places that they both loved and had visited before he lost his sight.

She shared these loved places with Tom and as she did, Tom joined in with his remembered images: they combined their individual recollections and associations. As they relived these treasures, Lily was surprised by the clarity and descriptive images of Tom's recall as well as how his memories had been maintained in surprisingly vivid technicolour detail. She said to him, "Your recollections are so much clearer and brighter than mine!" Weeks later, she told me how their experiences together had opened up deeper levels of communication, which neither of them had even considered before.

A number of my clients share many of their thoughts of gratitude with close family and friends, and they see how the happiness and even their enthusiasm spreads. One client described how she cuts up a gratitude thought list, folds each one and then puts them in a large, empty coffee jar. Then, when she and her friends are together, each one takes a thought from the jar and reads it out for everyone. This becomes a very uplifting way to enjoy tea or coffee together.

The Back of Your Journal
This part is for listening to, loving and understanding you

I recommend that you write in this part of your journal for around five or ten minutes early in your day.

Sometimes you can pick up cues or a gut feeling that someone else is distant or sad. When it seems appropriate, you may say, "Are you ok?" Then, when they respond, and you really listen to their problem respectfully… do you know that you gave them a gift? Do you sometimes ask yourself how you are and go inside to listen to your own thoughts? You can give yourself this same gift as you listen and write in the back of your journal for yourself.

The back of your journal is where you can freely off-load your thoughts. Whilst you write, you are completely focused and you are intently listening to yourself with love. And whilst you do this, you can pay closer attention to your needs. Any insight you gain can then be followed up if you wish to. These may well have the potential to free you to be true to yourself and to be wholeheartedly more open somewhere else in your life.

Writing in this part of your journal is a wonderful way to make time for you as well as to be your very own friend. While you are there for yourself, you may think of ways to consider some help for your up-till-now unspoken needs. When I really thought about this part of my journal, I realised that only I could possibly be there for me and only I could genuinely understand my feelings and reflect on what might be driving my reactions. I have discovered that this part of my journal requires a strong desire for truth and honesty together with zero judgement.

Writing a letter to someone in the back of your journal might work well for you. Just write and express your innermost thoughts, feelings and dreams – and include your worries too. This gives you the chance to feel heard as well as to learn what else is going on inside yourself. My clients tell me that even though the letter they wrote was never actually sent, doing this gave them more insight towards a possible way forward.

You may find that this can benefit a relationship or bring wisdom for a difficult meeting in the future.

When we acknowledge feelings and images as well as notice our inner chatter, we are able to understand ourselves more completely. Writing is a valuable way to express our needs so that we can find both new ways to be and novel actions we can take to make a difference. I have heard it said that, "What we don't acknowledge we can't change." Being more present within can bring us a far clearer perspective. If we ignore, push down or suppress our feelings, they can erupt inappropriately.

When I ignore or push down my feelings, I feel upset with myself for doing this, and my response just adds to my sadness. However, when I genuinely notice my own needs before they build up, I've observed that there is a major difference in how I handle situations. Both friends and clients have told me that really paying attention to what they feel inside has brought about major positive breakthroughs to their lives.

Many clients put their alarm on five minutes earlier than usual and have this important, loving and gentle five minutes of listening to their thoughts as they begin each new day. A number of people have told me that they choose an unusual place to do this – somewhere they wouldn't normally sit. This creates a neutral association for their writing, especially if they want to get something off their chest early each day in the back of their journal. I know someone who sits on the stairs every morning. Another person sits on the floor on a cushion. One client went and sat in the back of his car to write in the back of his book. He knew that choosing this place was a way for him to let go. He said his five minutes of paying attention to his thoughts and feelings was a really great start to every day.

The True Power of Our Intentions

"Whatever you can do, or dream you can begin it. Boldness has genius, power and magic in it."
Johann Wolfgang von Goethe

Journal reflections:

Ask yourself, "What do I need for me to be able to take the next step towards my desired choices?" As you sit with this question, allow time for past memories to surface – memories of taking worthwhile steps. Then write these intentions in the front of your journal.

If you wish to enjoy your life more freely, to relax and take things as they come, what indicators of this can you see? Where are the places and what are the times when you have felt at ease? Write these down in your journal. There will be suggestions and more examples in chapters 3 and 4 regarding this.

Chapter Two: A Brief Summary

In this chapter, you began to:
Write in your journal
Tap into the power of your desires
Create structures to support your intentions
Open your heart to the joy of gratitude
Listen to, love and understand you and your needs

CHAPTER THREE

Heart-centred ways to link hypnosis with your journal intentions

My very first experience of self-hypnosis

In 1974, when I was expecting my fourth baby, the National Childbirth Trust (NCT) recommended a book written by Erna Wright entitled *The New Childbirth*. It was intended for expectant mothers. For the birth of my three previous children, the NCT had encouraged me to practise a basic relaxation technique. These calming techniques were helpful for me in many ways. However, I had observed that as my contractions became more frequent and stronger, I found it was more difficult to relax.

After reading Erna's book and putting her techniques into practice, the benefits I received were much more consistent. This allowed my body and my baby to do what they were perfectly capable of achieving naturally and instinctively.

During my baby's delivery, my midwife asked me if I would be willing to experience one contraction without Erna's method. She told me that the NCT was interested in researching any added benefits, and she herself wanted to report back to them her own observed comparison of contractions both with and without this method. I was happy to do this, as it would give me the opportunity to report and monitor the help this new method gave to me.

During my next contraction, I used my previous basic relaxation techniques and soon realised that this contraction was very different. It felt as if the discomfort of the contraction was taking over. Then, on the next contraction and for the rest of my daughter's delivery, I used Erna's method. I felt calm and I had a feeling of going with the flow of my inner birth rhythm.

Following this beautiful birth, the midwife described to me the tremendous differences she noticed whilst I was using Erna's method. She said, "When you were using Erna's method, you easily got yourself out of your own way and allowed your baby's birth to happen naturally." This was exactly how I imagined it would be each time I visualized and practised throughout my pregnancy. This truly natural birth experience inspired me to research and learn more about our mind and body synchrony.

It was only after my daughter's birth that I realised Erna's book had been teaching me what I now believe to be self-hypnosis.

My self-hypnosis practice before my baby's birth

Self-hypnosis is a state of focused attention on something we are really wanting. And this is exactly what I did as I practised… Here is exactly what I did as I practised for my baby's delivery on most days leading up to her birth. I visualized, thought of, and imagined my feeling sensations through the process of my baby's birth. Then, I imagined myself resting easily when there were gaps between contractions. In my imagination, I went through each of the stages of her birth, and included welcoming my little one's arrival; I visualized everything going according to nature's plan.

I included in my practice listening and really paying attention to the sound of my midwife's voice, and her words of encouragement. Including this into my self-hypnosis practice was important for me, and for my baby's protection. If I had been too deeply relaxed, I might not have been able to access my midwife or doctor's instructions.

I also used relaxing breath-work to support and enhance the process of my letting go and allowing nature to take her beautiful course. I would imagine and enjoy doing this most days usually after lunch or just as I was drifting through self-hypnosis to sleep – always going all the way through and right up to the absolute joy of holding as well as feeding my little one.

Combining self-hypnosis practice with journal entry intentions

You can use self-hypnosis for an inspirational dream that you wish to bring to your life. Or, when you are following a particular desire that you feel very passionate about. It is your intention as well as your determination that connect you to your personal hypnotic journey. All hypnosis is self-hypnosis; it is not a sleep or unconscious state.

You frequently drift into a hypnotic trance state when you daydream. You may recall doing this? For example, I often go upstairs to get something and on my way up I completely forget what I was going up there for! At these times we have automatically drifted into a trance-like state. Many times a day we are going in and out of trance – our subconscious is running the show and in most circumstances doing this very successfully.

Research of children's brainwave patterns illustrate that young children between two to six years old are often in theta brainwave states. This state enables them to download phenomenal amounts of information they need so that they can thrive in their environment. Young children observe their environment and learn by watching, listening, using all their other senses, as well as practising consciously. Most of this learning is what we want, and also need, in later life for easy living. We really would not want to have to keep on relearning to walk! However, because of this amazing subconscious recording system, imagine the impact on a young child when they hear their parents say, "You will never amount to much," or other such comments. Once programmed into the subconscious, these comments can become truths that shape the behaviour and potential of a child.[1] Later in life, these memories can sometimes be automatically activated because the

---

[1]) Bruce H. Lipton PhD, *The Biology of Belief* Chapter 7 pages 170-174

subconscious believes protection is needed. However, if there is no real danger, just the discomfort of an old fear can be retriggered, or, if the triggering is strong enough, our stress response can be aroused. Some of my clients report that they are often hijacked by early unhelpful reactive patterns of responding. (These knee-jerk reactions are often called our conditioned responses.)

We are free now, if we want to, to make changes to these old, outdated patterns. Updating our subconscious responses is far more effectively achieved when we are in a trance or daydreaming state. These hypnotic dream states when combined with our conscious desires are powerful and will work cohesively together. They achieve calmer more self-confident responses; clients that I work with develop and change in areas where they have been stuck for many years. Our stuck states are frequently related to anxious memories and what we focus on we get more of. So, when we try and pull ourselves together consciously, it doesn't work because we are only using the conscious part of our brains.

When you wish to change an obsolete conditioned response, look for a desired intention from the front section of your journal. Then, whilst daydreaming or in a trance state, wander in your mind looking to find and connect to a time from early life (or last week) of a similar state of being. When you link these to your desires from the front of your journal, the synergy has the power to create new connections to your subliminal resources.

A client resolves his problem using an early memory

When he came to me, my client had severe public speaking anxiety – this had persisted for over two years. It began whilst presenting a team project to his colleagues. As he confidently gave an outline of the project, he happened to turn and catch sight of his manager's facial expression, and this unnerved him. After this, he was unable to face any public speaking events. So, with my help during our session, he went on a quest to find and use a time when he had been confident when speaking in public.

As a little boy, in the classroom, he recalled a specific moment when the teacher asked the class a question. He knew the answer and he clearly remembered being the first child to put his hand up and to answer the question correctly. Reconnecting to this reminded him of how confident he felt. His teacher was encouraging and even now he could picture, as well as feel, the kindness in her smile, and he heard in his mind exactly what she said to him. His recollection of this was a key find.

After making the link and recalling his teacher's encouragement, he regularly heard her words. He smiled as he saw her lovely smiling face, and he kept reminding himself of what she actually said. The repetition of his early memory came to mind last thing at night, as he relaxed and drifted gently off to sleep, and also when he woke up and at times throughout his day. His thoughts and the journal words he said to himself about this were "I communicate confidently and persuasively to groups now."

Two weeks after his appointment he rang excitedly to share how confident he had been when presenting an interesting suggestion to members of his team. Whilst doing this, he said he became very aware of how persuasive his suggestion had been when he saw how his team members reflected their own enthusiastic contributions back to him.

Getting started towards achieving worthwhile benefits for your life

Practising daydreaming and self-hypnosis yourself activates and reconnects you to specific feeling/memory states that relate to your journal's desired future intention. The fact that a feeling or memory you imagine is not identical to your intended scenario is not a problem. Your ideal desired state may have images, sounds, and excited gut feelings of knowing; can you connect to any of these? They have the potential to build trust for your growing purpose and this then creates an upbeat effect, closing the gap between your desired state and your future increasingly confident reactions.

This is the moment you link your resourceful state to your subconscious mind. When you consciously really want something and you connect to relevant associations, your imaginative practice of this empowered state opens up your heart-centred desires. When this happens, your passionate intentions fuse both conscious and subconscious minds harmoniously. This makes for perfect synchrony, taking you to the end results you are really wanting. Positive intentions, such as writing down inspiring words, touch a chord for your desired scenario, refreshing your positive memory recall of previously successful experiences. This action creates pathways in your brain. This is like any practice you have committed yourself to in your life before, and these gave you consistently positive results.

Integrating your inspiring journal associations with your self-hypnosis.

A client makes this happen in her own life

Clients often ask me how to make the most of the inspiring journal recollections that they have unearthed.

One client said she had recalled an event and then in the night following the same day in her dreams, she actually relived a glowing memory of her amazing high jump success. She was only ten years old at that time and yet, it was as exciting and vivid as ever, nearly twenty years later.

As she shared her experience with me, she talked much faster, and she became excited as she described the actual event as well as her dream associations to me. She was determined to re-imprint this powerful associated link because she knew it would be important for her. Over the next few weeks, she consistently reconnected to this euphoric state last thing at night. This is what she said to herself, "I frequently imagine and relive my fabulous high jump experience, each night, before dropping off, as well as when I awake." Her practice and positive intention to do her self-hypnosis just before going to sleep meant that it enabled her to develop added confidence in many areas of her life. The rehearsal of her remembered positive state meant that both her conscious and subconscious minds worked together perfectly.

How to use this for yourself at your highly suggestible times

Frequently our positive-state recollections come to mind as we link up to our heartfelt desires in our journal writing. Whenever upbeat states surface for you, it's valuable as well as crucial for you to explore your memorable recollections more deeply. Many clients use early photographs to help. And many discuss their recall with family and friends. When they do this, they find that everyone benefits from sharing these life-affirming happy times … and the recall itself is enriched.

You may see something or feel lighter or sense being carefree inside. As you continue to explore, you often remember the actual words that someone you loved or respected said to you. Now, as you make time to listen and notice how great it feels inside, you can be reconnecting to your sensations all over again. Taking your time, write this in the front of your journal – write what you saw as well as exactly how you felt. Sometimes you might become very aware of who was there at the time. As you calmly dig deeper, your recall may well come to you in even more detail.

Some clients think of how they would like to react – as if they were in somebody else's shoes. A lot of self-help books also recommend, "Fake it till you make it."

Do you have a friend or colleague who is positive and an absolute joy to be with? When you are with them does this lift you to another energetic level? Awareness of how you are in their company may give you happy feelings inside. Gifted speakers can also inspire us. This is why their seminars attract large audiences. The presenters' energy infuses us with wonderful vibes that take us to another level of imagining. Why not daydream upon their words and message when drifting off to sleep: this offers a wonderful boost to the energy of your personal intentions. As you do this, you may find that you will become a positive inspiration to others, too! If you are not able to take time to travel to seminars, you can listen to inspiring messages on Youtube from uplifting teachers and trainers.

Recently, a client described a technique she learnt to use which worked well for her. In her garden, she has an old stepladder, which she uses for her plant pots in the summer. It was winter, and as it was empty of pots, she decided to chalk up specific milestones she had recalled during her life that had been positively formative for her development in confidence. She ended up with inspiring keywords leading to the top step.

She started at the bottom with the first significant event that she clearly recalled. This was when her teacher asked the class to clear things from their desk. On the bottom rung, she wrote the exact words her teacher used: "Sally, you cleared up well." She said this to herself whilst she spent time reflecting through the first positive words she remembered. She was able to chalk up many other keywords, pictures and places, which tied into her neurology and they were all written on her ladder. Before the rain washed the words off the stepladder, she wrote them in the front of her journal. What surprised her most was how recalled words, images and experiences were continuously having a powerful effect on how good she felt all these years later.

We are different in the way that we unearth memories. Some of us may see images; many of us may have a felt, or kinaesthetic, sense that connects us to how things feel. Those who experience this sense often say they just know something is right: it is the inner feeling of balance even though they are unable to actually explain how they know. There are no right or wrong ways to explore your inner world. When you are playful and suspend your judgement, it certainly helps. Genuine interest and curiosity together with compassion can work well too. Why not practise unearthing your memories as you drift off to sleep, exploring your own senses such as taste, touch and smell – if these are part of your recollections. Then, as you sleep, you will be using all your imaginative links to seeing, feeling and hearing. These are all aspects of self-hypnosis.

We are also in highly suggestible hypnotic states when we begin to wake up. So, last thing at night and your early mornings are ideal moments to rehearse your day and night dreaming. As you link into your unique senses on a regular basis, you develop a new way of being. Whilst noticing these associations, you are actually building self-confidence, consolidating your progress and personal growth. Every day that you rehearse your desires you reconnect your brain to your personally confident states.

This is taken directly from Dr David Hamilton's book I Heart Me: **The Science of Self-love** (*In his Chapter Four - Visualization page 71*)

In summary - The brain doesn't distinguish between real and imaginary. Plenty of research shows that it changes as we do something and changes by about the same amount if we imagine doing the thing instead.

All elite athletes use this phenomenon of neuroplasticity to enhance their performance through visualization. Rehabilitation specialists also teach visualization to patients recovering from a stroke, because imagining movement actually helps the brain to recover.

What all this means is that we can imagine ourselves acting with a healthy level of self-worth and our brain will wire in this healthy level.

We can also forget how to have low self-worth, just as we can forget how to do long division. If we don't give our attention to thinking of ourselves as small or less-than and instead focus on thinking and acting in a way that's congruent with healthy self-worth, the brain networks connected with our lack of self-love will simply dissolve.

David's book also discusses the science surrounding our posture and our mind-body relationship. When we wish to feel confident, we can take a powerful upright posture, allowing our shoulders to relax down and back, whilst our head tilts slightly upwards. At times if it is appropriate, we could also place our hands on our hips. These postural changes all positively affect our brain so that we actually do feel more confident.

Thus, your imagining and the energy of your desire to receive whilst writing in your journal is the difference that makes the difference. Your conscious journal intentions, together with your remembered positive associations activate your life-affirming formula. Your consistent practice launches you in the direction that you are truly wanting. The energy of your desires plays a huge part towards moving towards what you wish for in your life. Whilst you practise in this way, both your conscious and subconscious minds work together – this is a winning combination.

Making Powerful Links to your own Inspiring Resourceful States

To access truly meaningful links to your powerful states, your desired intentions need to be crystal clear.

What is really important to you? Where in your own life do you absolutely wish to make a meaningful difference? Do you know exactly how your desired developments will inspire and help you? Is there an essential part of your life that really needs added confidence or a total change of direction from where you are currently heading? As you answer these questions or others, think of how you know that you need to move on, or change from your current course of action.

Go through the front section of your journal and highlight any must-have priority actions. Consider your memories again and really drill down. Maybe up until this time you have been unable to commit to your own life, your health and happiness, or even to your relationships with family, friends and colleagues. I believe that you and your life, as well as your health and happiness are a priority. It is natural to think of others and now, you need to be included too. And when you are, other benefits will fall into place. When you are happy and fulfilled, those around you feel this whilst being with you. The small daily steps you take, as you work with your journal, are ways to anchor these changes. One step at a time is a very good rhythm.

Making excellent use of the memories you have found takes you towards your unique way of utilizing information from your environment, from technology and the people you have contact with. This is an ongoing, automatic process within your brain and your body. The next few paragraphs ask you to consider these.

Whilst you read through the eight paragraphs below you may notice that one or two examples have more meaning, or they connect to your own unique way that you process or absorb information. I notice that some clients seem to favour visually based words like "I see" or "It looks beautiful." Or, for you, perhaps sound-based expressions connect with you such as "a robin singing" or "the church bell ringing". The expression "His conversation struck a chord" may relate to hearing or an intuitive knowing, or "a gut feeling". One client said that she was at ease inside when she said to herself "I just know this feels right for me."

As you look through these paragraphs, keep your journal handy to help with recall later. Make time for yourself, so that each paragraph has a chance – or not – to resonate with you. If a particular example means nothing at all or seems irrelevant, there is no need to consider that any further, just move onto the next one. Take a few moments and allow yourself to dream…

1.) Think of where you want to be, what you want or really desire to achieve in your life right now. Do you know what state is crucially important and highly relevant to your heart-centred intentions? When you feel a strong and passionate association, it will function like a laser beam focusing directly on what will automatically generate a workable connection to your innermost feelings. Even when this association is from some other situation or place, that's OK. When you come to review the association, and it resonates with you, it will often become clearer and stronger.

2.) Take a few moments and allow yourself to dream of an opportunity opening up for you. To build your energy, hold this thought, as well as an awareness of exactly what would encapsulate experiencing fulfilment. This could be a recollection of a specific time when you felt in a naturally productive state or a wonderful experience when you easily flowed with life. Be kind: relax and take a while to pick up feelings or memories in your body. Some people say they find themselves beginning to smile.

Then, imagine you are looking around for a friend to talk to about this. Just guess at someone being right there who is well placed and willing to bounce ideas around with you. This someone is a person you already respect who has helped you, and you them. You have been through interesting times together and you completely trust and respect one another. Imagine hearing your conversation together and the excitement building in your voices.

3.) Is it important for you to change a present or future situation? Do you want a specific positive association now or at some time in the future? As you consider this, how would you define what state or way of responding is important for you? Right now, take a moment and revisit special places and times in your memory. As you do this, write down some words, locations, dates or people's names. These can be rough notes: they will serve to help you remember some of these positive fleeting memories. When you come to review your notes, you will be able to create a number of worthwhile associations to memory pathways. Thinking through them strengthens these snapshot associations, and when you need them, they will be readily accessible at exactly the right time for you.

4.) If you are someone who is very visual, you probably often see or dream in pictures. Maybe faces pop into your mind and places you have visited come to you really easily. As you see yourself at the beach, perhaps you can feel the sandy grit when picking up and washing pebbles and shells; the water flowing over your toes feels delicious. When you travel in your memory or in your imagination, you'll be making the images familiar for you in the future. This rehearsal process means that you are practising in your mind, as well as within your body.

5.) You may have a photographic memory for words, maps and books that you have read. You might recall photos of people or precise details of places you have been to. If so, where will you go or who will you see and what will you do in your imagination as you think of yourself finding and creating a more inspiring life?

6.) Are you someone who is transported by the taste of a deliciously nourishing meal, or someone who loves to spend time just relaxing with a drink? When you recall, for example, an exotic ginger sweet or the pleasurable sensations of an Italian tangy ice cream, what is going on inside? Is it the initial icy hit that awakens you, as it melts with the delight of lime on your tongue? If, however, you prefer savoury experiences, how about a colourful, taste-bud tingling and delightfully hot and out-of-this-world oriental curry that delights your palate. As you do this, you will be exploring oceans of opportunities that you'll be able to use whenever you wish.

7.) Smells can be very evocative and frequently link with other associations to bring insight when we wish to connect to something really magical again. When I asked one client for recall of pleasant places or happy events she looked completely blank. Then I said, "Do you have some lovely aroma memories?" As her mind slowly wandered through and around this, I watched a dramatic transformation take place of the whole of her body and her face. She looked really calm and happy. She told me that in her granny's garden there was a lavender path leading to the little potting shed. She really loved brushing past those little bushes when she was a little girl to pick up the gorgeous scent. She described how connecting to her lavender memories helped to lift her, bringing calm. From then on, she frequently used this to change her state.

8.) Sounds can be evocative too. Do you have memories of the rain going pitter-patter on a roof or beating on your windowpane? As you hear the rain in your imagination, do you feel snug, warm and cosy inside? Or are there uplifting songs that, earlier in your life, you listened to that, as you listen today can still transport you back to those great times once again? Many clients say they love to hear the background sounds of the seashore on their hypnosis recordings. Some say it reminds them of early holidays or a day at the beach. Each of these may be a pleasurable association that is very personal and unique. Whilst thinking of memories connected to happy sounds it is worthwhile linking all these sound associations together so that they lift you to pleasanter levels and enrich your wellbeing.

If just one of the above paragraphs connects you to a happy enjoyable memory association, it would be well worth exploring that one in even more detail. Do you remember how my client's childhood memories of her grandma's lovely lavender bushes could frequently take her to happier states just by thinking about their aroma? The same kind of thing can happen for you when you too wander in your own imagination and discover a simple memory association unique to you.

Here is a similar early childhood experience which another client shared with me. This was of a time on holiday when he was a little boy. He related to me how, as he was half asleep, his grandfather very gently lifted him out of his bed. He then carried him carefully across the sand and they sat together on top of a rock and looked at the sparkling night sky. He told me how he felt his grandfather's joy as he showed him the dramatic night sky shimmering across the sea. As this client talked to me about this early life experience, he knew he still was emotionally inspired some forty years later, and he realised that this amazing memory would uplift him many more times again.

Now is the very best time for you to gather together any little associations of joy and memorabilia that have been stirring within you. These nuggets and associations are more valuable than gold. They are gifts given to you from other times and experiences in your life that need to be treasured and written within your journal so that they are there to cherish and nourish you again.

Journal Reflection Point – Ways I perceive my world

As you read through your journal, you may start to notice the words which pop up often. Awareness of these can offer you other choices. Fresh ideas that come will surprise you and advance your growing desire to stretch yourself and seek novel ways to think, feel, and express yourself as you push back your vocabulary and sensory boundaries. This offers you a wealth of information.

A simple way of owning a fresh vocabulary in your journal and in your life is to use different coloured pens to highlight. These can alert you to the representational system you are aware of and use. For instance, words which relate to seeing, imagining or visualizing could be highlighted in red so you would stop and think of how you express these and you can easily incorporate them in your life.

The words related to sounds could be in blue. You could then highlight in blue in your journal anything related to this modality. Then, when you think of blue highlighting, this will alert you to your auditory communications that you are using in external and internal conversation and whilst writing in your journal.

Your kinaesthetic words could be highlighted in yellow. This modality relates to feelings as well as bodily sensations. Many people find it is hard to differentiate their awareness of these. Sometimes questions help: What is it like to feel wool next to my skin? Or what is it like for me to taste a spoonful of salty soup?

Your gustatory representation is all about the sense of taste: sweet, salty, as well as sour flavours. I suggest an orange highlighter here. Tastes also relate to sights, sounds and pictures (as do smells), and these will filter into your awareness, enrich your life and impart varied colourful levels of perceiving.

As we reach the end of Chapter 3, I look forward to imagining that your world of experience during these journal-reflected perceptions will offer you glowing insights – you may even find yourself sharing your experiences with others!

Chapter Three: A Brief Summary

In this chapter, you:
Learnt how to incorporate your journal desires into your life
Were introduced to the power of visualizing when drifting off
Discovered how impressionable you are when waking early
Found out how your inner knowing reveals your life-affirming gifts
Looked for positive memories and physical senses that create results
Imagined viable experiences that could work wonders for you

CHAPTER FOUR

The Bridge Technique

In my early practice during the 1980s, clients and I were incorporating hypnosis with regression to clear their disturbing events. I became aware of interesting changes that occurred at some times. It was clear that fewer therapy appointments were required. Clients were noticing they were able to interact more confidently with others, or they no longer wished to smoke; those who wanted to eat more healthily were finding it easier to do so. However, I was surprised when clients reported that their physical or emotional distress no longer played a part in their lives. I was puzzled and also determined to research this by going through client notes. I followed up a random selection of clients to see if their benefits remained stable.

With few exceptions, clients had continued to progress well. In a large proportion of these notes, many of these clients had beliefs that they had received abilities and gifts before conception and sometimes at their birth. I hypothesised that these beliefs, together with an intuitive sense of recovering their birthright meant that there would be no reason, need or desire to rewrite history, as we had often done. Rather, I thought, that if the client reconnected with these gifts when going back in time during hypnosis, conclusive benefits would be gained.

A number of clients described their experience as receiving their unique gifts or as a wonderful feeling of belonging. Others said, "I now have feelings of being whole or complete." After five years of randomised research I saw that a complete release of a trauma happened far more frequently in certain specific circumstances. With few exceptions, the difference between noticeable benefits and fewer improvements seemed to relate to some of the post-hypnotic suggestions that were given.

Many of these post-hypnotic suggestions corresponded to a client's new-found beliefs and expectations of reconnecting to the way they were born to be. At other times, the significant improvement was a synchronisation of their mind, body, heart and soul as they accessed a meaningful resourceful past experience. The catalyst to client freedom seemed to be a reconnection that linked them to a time before their difficulties. Their gift of completeness appeared to be held in the archives of their minds.

The clients' heart-centred intentions seemed to be creating a bridge to their specific histories. One client who had been arthritic for years said, "I believe that my mind and body know how my pre-arthritic body functioned and it is still there for me now." Others said that what was happening came from an earlier point in time before they ever experienced a difficulty or trauma. Those who experienced the dramatic changes reported that they intuitively knew what they were wanting and believed that it already belonged to them. These reports were truly inspirational to me, and the results pointed to massive shifts in their lives.

Some clients who required fewer appointments told me that there were measurable changes in their confidence in their lives. Others said that their current independence was a truly healthy way to be. One very measurable change came from a couple who had been receiving a number of fertility treatments. When they were eventually told by the clinic that they were incompatible, they were distraught. They experienced a very close connection with one another and so they stopped their IVF treatment because they just didn't believe what they were told. Some months later after treatment with hypnosis, the woman became pregnant without any IVF treatment. This was very likely due to the activation through the couple's own beliefs, intentional desire, expectancy as well as trust in the ability to choose their unique connection to their own completeness.

Be consistently true to yourself

From my research, it became clear that a reconnection to clients' firmly held trust and beliefs balanced their lives:

- Clients expressed a strong desire for, and really wanted, the freedom to feel the way they were before their problem or trauma had occurred
- Their heart and soul's passionate intention was obvious to both of us
- Clients expressed to me their expectancy of being whole again and they trusted themselves deeply
- Their energy of asking was very strong whilst going back in time.
- They expressed appreciation as well as an emotional welcome back to the gifts given to them at their conception.

I also found that giving clients a post-hypnotic suggestion before they left, was an effective mechanism that allowed them to retain their insightful learning and move on in their lives. I recorded precise wording for clients during their hypnosis. They were then more likely to retain the learning whilst they were in a suggestible state. Their transformative experiences were consolidated within their hearts, minds and bodies.

The Development of The Bridge Technique

In early 2000 after training with Gary Craig, the developer of EFT (Emotional Freedom Techniques), I began to research the possibility of creating a reconnection whilst using EFT in a similar way to my hypnotherapy practice. I was interested in combining the benefits of both of these self-help therapies.

Whilst clients and I were working with EFT, I noticed that they were frequently in a trance state. Many clients were keen to explore the benefits of combining EFT with a trance state to help them in their lives, and their joint desire – the client's intention and their need to let go of past hurts – activated this manifestation.

(EFT, a powerful stand-alone therapy, will be explored in more depth in Chapter 6.)

Since working in this way, clients have continued with surprisingly beneficial effects. Combining gentle acupressure touch on acupoints instead of traditional tapping on the EFT acupoints and using the clients' words including hypnotic language patterns, appears to be the ideal process to use. I am always led by my clients' desired intention of what they are wanting, as this opens the way for the best possible outcome available for each and every one.

In 2009, a number of my case history experiences were published in a chapter of the book called *EFT & Beyond – Cutting Edge Techniques for Personal Transformation*; the book, edited by Pamela Bruner and John Bullough, includes innovative ideas from twenty-seven internationally acclaimed experts. I have included a copy of my chapter in the Appendix.

Reconnecting you to your birthright can help you physically

The development of The Bridge Technique started when clients came with physical problems such as blushing, hay fever and pain. (I require in all cases that clients receive medical checks before using hypnosis or other therapies. Frequently doctors recommend clients to me when there is no known physical reason for their clients' problem.) During the course of working with clients I have discovered that having a positive intention and asking for a reconnection to a time in their life before they developed their physical discomfort would often help relieve their problem. I observed that this process released fears and possibly the emotional memory component of their injury, which may have been impacting on their inner wisdom to heal.

The Bridge Technique is frequently successful with the treatment of smoking and other addictive cravings or behaviour

When I am with a client who wants to stop smoking, we talk about the fact that, within the memory archives of smokers, they were born as a non-smoker. This freedom of living without cigarettes is our birthright. Therefore, before they began to smoke there was no reason, need or desire to do so.

Thus, when any one of us starts smoking for whatever reason, the brain still retains the programme of being born free and complete in every way as a non-smoker. In view of this, I have found that when clients come and consciously decide that now they want to let go of their need to smoke, the most helpful process is not to create a void by taking cigarettes away or stopping them from smoking. A simpler and more effective process is to go through the procedure of making a reconnection to the way that client was before they ever started smoking. Clients report feeling happy as a non-smoker and even describe themselves as feeling reborn, once again receiving their gift of complete freedom as a non-smoker. They often report that the reconnection experience gives them feelings of liberation and they end up celebrating what they have learnt.

Journal reflection:

As you read this now, you too may wonder where you would like to go for a healthy reconnection for yourself. Your thoughts and feelings about this can be written in the front of your journal. Take a while to wonder – there is no rush – and guess at exactly what you would want most for yourself whilst you link up to memory associations. For example, what times or places do you recall enjoying energetic health? Did you love a sport, gardening or some other lively activity? Where do you wish to experience the joy of freedom in life now? What would you choose to be or to do?

Sift through associations of times when, for example, you were keen on cycling with the wind in your hair or swimming with the waves lifting you. (Have you come up with an experience similar to these – or something else entirely?)

In a calm state of mind, imagine a time, choosing from among the associations you made just before this. This pleasantness naturally links to enjoyable feelings and to other decisions and intentions you want to follow. This is the art of right thinking – it is part of the fun of challenging and leading ourselves forward as we continue in our lives. The absolutely best time to do this, as we've already seen, is as you drift into sleep or just as you wake. Make an intention to recall a happy memory and think of feeling light and carefree again in a similar way to how you were in earlier parts of your life.

Benefits can also be captured for those who wish to be free to let go of addictive desires for retail therapy or gambling – or, we may perhaps wish to drink less coffee or enjoy healthy amounts of alcohol. Asking for serenity gives us the passionate desire to let go and reconnect to the essence of who we really are. Your own heartfelt desire to move towards a vivacious life is available for you too. When you are passionate about living life on purpose then whatever you wish to reconnect to in terms of healthy living is also available to you in the archives of your mind.

At another time when you pick up and read this book again, you may want to access specific interests and unique associations for yourself. No one needs to know what you are following through with except yourself. When you support yourself with dreams of genuinely upbeat decisions, you may well feel deep inside a warmth glowing and that is a great help in your determination.

Stories of how others have reconnected to their confident and healthy independent resources

This reconnection is an energetic process that is both intuitive and simple to do. It has the power to completely change our state of being. It takes us from lethargy towards personal empowerment. Here I share with you four brief, true stories. (Throughout this book, personal details have always been changed to respect and protect each person's identity.)

Claire's story

Claire came to me because she was experiencing panic attacks. These distressed her and meant that her confidence was being eroded in places or circumstances that brought on her attacks. She really loved her life and was passionate about what she experienced in her work as a support teacher in a special needs nursery – she was respected by the children, their parents as well as her colleagues. She described what she did at work as her calling. However, on the day she came for help, she said she felt unable to continue: her manager's continual criticism was chipping away at her confidence.

When she talked to me about her work with the youngsters that she looked after, her face lit up with love. She was remembering one particular breakthrough experience with a child and this memory was a bright light, which really stood out in her life.

Claire had developed and implemented unique innovations and one of these was a special 'thrive room' as a 'time out' place to go to for these little ones when in need. The calm of this room meant it released their distress. On the day in question, this very challenged little boy made a major breakthrough and everything came together. At the same time this happened, all the parents had arrived to collect their little ones as it was home-time. Everyone just stood around open-mouthed in sheer amazement as they witnessed this little one's transformation.

We used the experience of this life-changing association during hypnosis as a catalyst for her to connect to her naturally powerful state again. Recalling what happened on a particular day with a very withdrawn child taught her to see, as well as really hear again, the joy of this little boy's laughter, and to reconnect to her own self-confidence. We created a recording together of her story that included gentle EFT touch with hypnosis for her to take home.

When Claire came to see me again, she said, "If this little boy can overcome his fears, then I can certainly do the same!" She just knew that her manager would never ever have the power to intimidate her again.

George's story

George had spent many years drifting since leaving school – he seemed to have lost his way. With no purpose in his life, he had turned to drugs and they only added to his problem. When I asked him to tell me about highlights from his life, he thought for a considerable time and then his energy state lifted as he talked about a specific music teacher who had taken him under her wing. His recollections of all that she had helped him to do bathed him anew with the same lovely feelings he had felt then. This memory recollection energized him and allowed him to be truly animated. After he learnt how to reconnect to this empowering memory, he was able to make more healthy choices in his life. One day during his appointment he said to me, "My music teacher invested time and an unshakable belief in me as a musician. I will now continue to remember exactly what I learnt and instil that same feeling and belief she inspired in me through frequent recall."

Pete's story

Pete came to me because he had seen how a therapy appointment with me had changed one of his dear friends overnight. As he described his problem to me, he became emotional when he said "whenever there are people around me." There were tears in his eyes and he became very anxious and was having difficulty in continuing. It became clear that the presence of others around or being in crowds had always upset him. I gently suggested that he allow his eyes to close whilst he listened to some seashore sounds on my recording system. As he listened, he visibly relaxed and let go. I asked him, "Can you see anything?" His reply "Yes, and it's beautiful." I allowed him to continue his relaxation and after a while I said "You came here for a reason. Whatever it was you wanted, will you imagine it coming to you because you came here to ask for this?" Pete just nodded and smiled as in a dream.

Over time, I have noticed that when someone genuinely and sincerely asks, they receive. After a while I said to him, "Have you received what you came here for?" For quite a while, he continued to calmly relax – the gentle seashore background was still playing. When he opened his eyes, he said he was excited that he had received benefits for himself. His focused intention was a very important factor in what had happened. As we talked, he combined gentle EFT touch on some of his face points. Very quickly he became much more coherent and upbeat. Then, spontaneously, he began recalling events and times when he clearly felt free. He described his family, friends and even how he pictured his life then and how he expected it to be that way when he left me and from then on.

I received a card from Pete after he went away with his family. This is what he wrote:

> *"To Mary,*
>
> *I recently went on holiday to Switzerland and discovered how little the crowds of people bothered me. So, I send this card as a 'thank you' for all the support you gave me last summer because it's really worked wonders!*
>
> *From Pete"*

Positive expectations are valuable assets: they support and inspire us

Our positive expectations are inspirational states. They nourish and cherish us. Each of us has a kernel of desire that needs nurturing, and friends and family can help nurture that if they really listen. When they do, their interest shines a light to help us. When we share happy experiences from the past and the present with others, those seeds are activated again. Then, whenever we tend and water them, they flower and brighten up our lives – so much more than we could have predicted.

Alex's story

Alex, a delightfully friendly young man, came for help to clear his early experiences of physical abuse. This destructive legacy hampered both his enjoyment of loving closeness with his partner and his sexual freedom. His painful memories held him back from ever initiating intimacy. However, when his partner gently and lovingly encouraged him, he could relax and feel safe. Otherwise, he always felt himself holding back – there were so many painful images and his feelings overwhelmed him.

He had embarked on a number of therapies; however, these feelings continued to be a sticking point for him. During his first appointment, we explored non-related times of freedom – of running barefoot through grass as a little child or of diving confidently into a friend's swimming pool. Neither of these pleasant experiences gave him the energy required to change his stuck state.

What looks like a block could well be a chance to be free

On his second appointment, he was happy to explore a combination of EFT and hypnosis to bring about a reconnection to the freedom he had felt in very early life. Half way through this process, he became really excited: he just knew something important had happened to him.

He told me that as a child, he frequently stayed at his grandparents' farm and when he was there, he often rode his horse. His excitement grew as he told me that whenever he was there, he knew that he could jump on his horse anytime he wished.

The memory of being able to do this whenever he felt like it was the key that liberated him from his trauma. He found he only had to imagine his horse and the freedom he felt as a very little boy: and he was reconnected with his freedom as an adult. He understood he could choose what he wanted and he felt he would make that decision. The combination of EFT and The Bridge Technique brought him what he wanted.

What you have just read are specific examples of others' experiences which have transformed them. They found liberation for themselves through their memories from earlier times in life, and this made real sense. The examples of times like these could be there within you for you too. Of course, yours will be different. You may have to dig a little, as my clients did, but that's normal.

Journal reflections:

What are you thinking of writing in your journal for this chapter?

Before you leave, I'll indulge my curiosity and ask you, "Did any of the brief stories in this chapter create a connection to or for you?" If one or more did, how could you link this to your developing commitment to yourself? Writing it down helps to make it stick.

Chapter Four: A Brief Summary

In this chapter, you:
Imagined 'The Bridge Technique' giving you choices
Thought of confidently using your own resources
Found your own gifts and welcomed them
Recalled calming ways to be kind to yourself
(Did someone's story resonate for you? If so, do look at it again.)

PART TWO

DISCOVERING
Finding, and Accepting You

CHAPTER FIVE

The miracles of the mind-body connection

A little science background

It has been enormously helpful, for me and my clients, to make sense of why we experience emotions and feelings. Understanding what is happening in our mind and body opens up fresh choices that we can make. Finding our own way from not knowing how this is happening towards more clarity, opens up practical ways for us to make changes and develop better coping strategies.

Making sense of stress and our fear reactions in life

The sympathetic nervous system activates the stress response within the limbic system: a part of our brain connected to the autonomic nervous system.

Stress responses are intended to protect as well as take care of us. When we are on the receiving end of these reactions, they can disrupt our sleep, digestion, and our immunity. This happens when our subconscious thinks our life is in danger, and stress hormones such as adrenalin and cortisol are produced to give us energy fuel to save our lives. They help us to fight, to take flight or freeze.

Moving through unhelpful emotions and reactions in your life

Dr Joe Dispenza's book *You Are The Placebo* states on page 118 "Studies show that getting in touch with positive, expansive emotions like kindness and compassion – emotions that are our birthright, by the way – tends to release a different neuropeptide (called oxytocin), which shuts off the receptors in the amygdala, the part of the brain that generates fear and anxiety. With fear out of the way, we can feel infinitely more trust, forgiveness, and love. We move from being selfish to selfless. And as we embody this new state of being, our neuro-circuitry opens the door to endless possibilities that we never could have even imagined before, because now we're not expending all our energy trying to figure out how to survive."

Introducing the vagus nerve

I was fascinated when I first heard about the vagus nerve from someone who had felt anxious in very specific situations. Occasionally they passed out due to associations that were triggering them sub-consciously. Around 80–90% of the nerve fibres of the vagus are used to communicate the state of our internal organs to our brain. For instance, if we have tension in our gut, this is transmitted from our internal organs to the brain through sensory fibres. Vagal tone is the level of change occurring in the parasympathetic nervous system that affects our heart rate function. It keeps our heartbeat within a safe range. When the tone of this nerve increases or reduces we feel changes in our heart rate.

The vagus nerve fibres are also connected to the motor and autonomic nervous system. This nerve, then, is not only sensory fibres; sometimes it is called the wandering nerve because it has connections throughout our body. It is not only a bottom up from gut to brain but also a top down communication process, through which our brain instructs the gut to create a state for rest and digestion when we feel calm and safe, as well as instructions to fight or take flight when dangers are around us. What interests me about this nerve is that this action takes place in a completely subconscious way and therefore is unrelated to our thinking. Action occurs more on the level of body awareness.

That's why sometimes we are unable to make sense of why we feel anxious when there appears to be no reason for anxiety. The vagus plays an important role both in the sympathetic nervous system which is activated within us at difficult or dangerous times and in the transitions to the parasympathetic nervous system which allows us to return to relaxation and recovery.

In addition, higher vagal tone also fluctuates depending on our social relationships, and how we react to others' pain or discomfort. This means that our own kind and compassionate responses to others change our vagal tone. This can also affect the vagal tones of those we come in contact with.

Understanding the role of the vagus in this process and finding ways to support it, means we can work on emotional tuning and on self-control. An excellent way to act on vagal tone is related to its regulatory function of breathing and heart rate variability. Our breathing, when deep and slow, involves the movement of the diaphragm and that is important. When our out-breath is longer than our in-breath this lowers our heart rate. This way of breathing can be a great help before or during a stressful situation because it immediately fine-tunes the vagal response. That is why practices such as yoga and meditation are associated with better vagal tone.

At times that are not life-threatening, as when your boss is giving you critical feedback after a meeting or when you feel anxious whilst out with friends, the sudden appearance of a fight-or-flight level of anxiety is extremely unhelpful to say the least. One of my intentions in this book is to share with you ways for you to re-assure as well as re-educate the part of your brain that can be hijacked by old fears. It is possible that our brain is still hanging onto outdated subconscious reactions that may no longer have relevance or usefulness to us now.

If you received unfair criticism from someone or you were bullied at school, trying to pull yourself together consciously unfortunately doesn't work to alleviate your anxiety. Our responses are automatically linked to anything that remotely reminds the subconscious part of our brain of previous painful experiences. So if you are being criticised today by your manager, the history of that experience of unfair criticism at school could well trigger you. As you encourage a return to calmer states, your longer slower breath out relaxes you.

Journal Experience

A small percentage of our reactions don't make us feel safe or relaxed, so considering these with kindness rather than ignoring them or condemning them will actually be the beginning of better things to come. A good habit to get into is writing about these in your journal, invoking kindness as you do so.

First, make a note of the reactions you would love to be free of. After this, ask yourself exactly what you would prefer to say and do instead – even if it's a stretch. This opens you up to fresh choices because we are what we think. Then, when you notice yourself on the road to moving beyond these obsolete reactions, you also notice many wonderful changes occurring. As you see these changes taking place, you see the real evidence – what is actually happening – of your ever-growing self-belief and feelings of confidence.

Your conscious mind's responses

As you read along, the conscious part of your mind is probably analysing what I have written here. What you think about it relates to your own unique experiences in life. However, an enormous part our lives is happening automatically at the subconscious level – and at that level, we are not living on purpose. I want to open doors and introduce strategies to you that lead you towards increased awareness of your inner conversation. If you are aware that what you are thinking is distressing you, then you have the opportunity to gently steer yourself towards desires and away from the unhelpful inner chatter. Many clients wear a band or bracelet on their wrist, which they gently flick as a reminder to become conscious of subconscious responses and to move towards what is important for them. You might want to experiment with this.

All your consistently tiny daily steps in the right direction add to your confidence, thoughtful action, and your healthy self-expression.

Therefore, when you feel reactions in your body or you notice thoughts that come to you, you can ask yourself a question such as "Is this thought helpful or is it harmful to me?" Your answer to this question gives you a chance to decide to keep that thought or to let it go.

As things begin to be more meaningful, you can increasingly enjoy more healthy independence. Our genuine interest, compassion and kindness towards ourselves has been proved to be good for our health and happiness. David Hamilton's book *The Five Side Effects of Kindness* will offer you scientific reasons for why this is good.

Your subconscious conditioned responses

If a part of your brain remembers being lost for words, whilst you are giving a presentation or you are in an interview, you may well go into a freeze response. This stress reaction is meant to protect you from embarrassment again, however, it may well hamper your chances of inspiring your audience. Many people who are professional speakers today have had to go through making adjustments to their own outdated conditioned responses. If we have no desire or intention to move on from an embarrassing experience we would continue to struggle. If we are determined to put that behind us, our decisive intention restores and builds our confidence to another level. These incredible benefits mean, for example, that we become a sought-after and inspirational speaker because we know, and have felt, the challenging ups and downs too. Without these negative experiences, we would not have the confidence to share our own vulnerability, and doing this can be an enormous help to others who will benefit from us actually expressing our learning.

Journal experience

Right now, can you think of someone's infectious laughter? As you remember it, you may laugh again. Just thinking about this can change your state. When you apply images, sounds, or words of an upbeat song that felt fabulous at the time, you remember the euphoria again. Practise this switching from upbeat to stuck states again... and perhaps again. Write out a powerful desired state you want or have already experienced in the front of your journal. Then recall or explore what you want to move away from. This could be from the back of your journal. The practice of thinking or feeling these opposite experiences will make it easier for you to connect up again.

Observing how our thoughts affect our physical responses

Following my study, training and research into Energy Therapy Techniques as well as the current science background of our mind-body relationship, I was still passionate and excited to delve in more deeply. The following study illustrates interconnections between thoughts and feelings and just how our thoughts and feelings affect our physiology.

I was introduced to a biofeedback machine in 1999 and I have used it on myself and with my clients. They find it intriguing as well as helpful when they use it on themselves. It clearly illustrates how their calm or anxious thoughts have an effect on their physical stress levels. Using this has been particularly helpful when clients worry about their health, finances or relationships. You may well wonder how this may help you too. If you are interested in finding out more about this machine, there is a reference to this in the resource section at the back of this book.

How a biofeedback machine helped a client regarding his worries about his health

Ryan's chest consultant recommended that he come to see me for stress management training – he had high BP.

His worries were related to a frightening experience that, to him, felt like a heart attack. However, after that experience, all of his tests in hospital were returned to him and he was given a clean bill of health. His local GP was still monitoring his BP, which continued to be high.

At his first consultation, Ryan described how worried he was about his high BP. He told me that he thought that somehow, something had been overlooked. It had to be the case; otherwise, why would his BP still be high? We discussed the stress response and then I asked him if he could describe to me some of the relaxing, peaceful places he had been to. He obviously enjoyed this and relaxed considerably.

Because I really wanted Ryan to be comfortable with the idea of this machine before using it with him, I told him how my students always loved watching the changes in the readings on this machine when they are using it. On one particular occasion, after a while of experimenting with it on themselves, one of them said, "Can we put it on you, Mary?" Of course that was ok with me until they started teasing and goading me about the high readings, and then they began to wonder out loud why I might be embarrassed! Then they said, "You would think that Mary could relax easily; isn't that what she teaches other people to do?"

My story of being put on the spot seemed to relax Ryan because he asked if he could try it on himself. He said he would be very interested to see how his thoughts and understandable worries could have been affecting his stress levels and in turn his BP readings. I recommended that he think of his most peaceful place at the lake fishing and only to glance down occasionally at the monitor. I also suggested that he could let his thoughts wander around these pleasant times and then to wander to his worry thoughts and back again to the fishing lake.

I asked him if it was ok with him if I left the room whilst he explored the effects of his thoughts. (I do this whenever it is appropriate so that clients won't feel under pressure to perform for me.) Ryan was comfortable with me doing that.

When I returned to my consulting room, he told me how fascinating it was to just sit there, not move, and to see that just by changing his thoughts, the monitor went up or down. He left in a much more positive frame of mind after a brief session of hypnosis, which included reiterating his experience and suggesting that he would be feeling much calmer about his health on his next visit to his doctor.

Ryan came back to see me two weeks later and reported that his BP was now normal. He said his GP had asked him what he had been doing since his last appointment. He told his GP what he had been thinking about whilst he was having his BP taken. Then he explained to me exactly what he had done before he went to his doctor. The night before his BP test, just before drifting off to sleep, he imagined that the monitor he had used with me was going down to a relaxed level just as he had watched it in my consulting room. Seeing how his thoughts were both activating and alleviating his stress response impressed him greatly; knowing this gave him the tools to be able to help himself in his present and in the future.

Can you think of a time when you too were able to switch your thoughts away from a problem? Did you find novel ways of clearing the intensity of how you felt? Ryan imagined a lake. What did you imagine? As you do this with pleasant thoughts, notice how good it is to be less intense.

Journal reflections:

In the front of your journal, write a story about you sharing an exciting change you have created in your life.

If it is easier for you, think of telling your story to an imaginary friend. Explain how this actually happened and what led to the success of your venture. Do that now or sketch it out as a picture.

In the front of your journal, write down a desire you are intending to achieve in your life. Then in a colourful way describe how you believe this will actually happen.

Picture yourself taking steps, making contacts, carrying out research. Give yourself a moment to consider exactly what you still need to achieve that will allow events to fall into place.

Then, using your imagination, write down how you are walking towards and meeting exactly the right people to collaborate with you and help make your dream happen. Do this with conviction – right deep down inside yourself.

Chapter Five: A Brief Summary

In this chapter, you dived into:
Discovering mind/body connection miracles
Science background to enhance awareness of free choice
Ways to move past the stress response
Improving vagal nerve tone
How giving and receiving kindness releases happiness hormones

CHAPTER SIX

Emotional Freedom Techniques (EFT)

In the next three chapters, three energy therapies are discussed. For more details from the developers of EFT, TAT, and BSFF, visit their website addresses which are included at the end of each therapy technique.

In the 1990s, my husband Tam and I learnt about EFT through some videos a dear colleague lent us. The videos were recorded by Gary Craig, the developer, at the Veterans Administration Center in Los Angeles. These were deeply moving and illustrated EFT's transformative results. After watching these dramatic recoveries from the Vietnam veterans' PTSD traumas, I suddenly knew with results like these, I owed it to my clients to learn and to train in this wonderful self-help technique. My passion has always been to offer healthy independence. EFT was certainly a simple technique that offered this.

Tam and I trained with Gary and we eventually became EFT Founding Master Practitioners. In 2005 Tam invited Gary Craig to present an EFT seminar in the UK. Five hundred people from 25 different countries attended. Following this, there was a huge expansion of EFT across Europe and elsewhere.

For additional details, visit Gary Craig's website: www.emofree.com where there are many case histories, stories and other resources. Here, you can also subscribe to Gary Craig's newsletters for added support and information.

Why EFT works well on the emotions that are blocking us

What we don't acknowledge or what we choose to ignore we cannot change. EFT, because of its ability to connect to the energy of our emotions, gives us access to enormous depth of growth and development in that area. So, when we notice we are feeling ecstatically high or emotionally flat, these high and low energy times open doors to that deeper connection; they are brilliant opportunities to do our EFT tapping work on ourselves. When we experience seeds of possible opportunities and much wider fields to explore, often our fear of failure washes the seeds down the drain. As we gain more confidence in EFT, we discover tapping helps enormously when we treat our fears. EFT lets us know that the opportunities are really there just for the asking. Each time we use the tapping, it opens a window to beautiful changes that are waiting to happen inside ourselves.

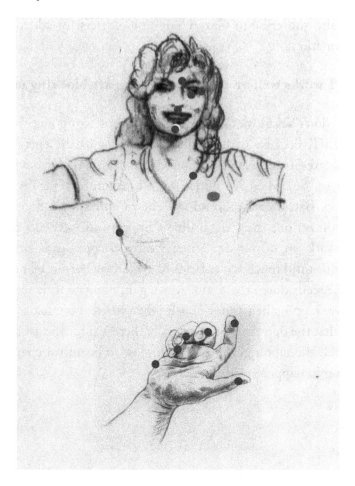

From the diagram, you will notice that all the tapping points are in easily accessible places. The tapping is usually carried out with two fingers together, the index finger and the middle finger. (Two fingers cover a larger area ensuring we connect to the acupressure point.)

The Steps of EMOTIONAL FREEDOM TECHNIQUES

1.) Scale the Problem from 1 – 10 SUDs (Subjective Unit of Distress)

2.) **Tap the karate chop point** [2] **and say the following three times.**

"Even though I.......... (name problem), I deeply and completely accept myself anyway." (This is called the reminder phrase)

3.) **Tap each of the following points 7 times as you state the reminder**

Eyebrow, Side of Eye, Under Eye, Under Nose, Chin, Collarbone, Under Arm, Thumb, Index Finger, Middle Finger, Ring Finger, Little Finger, Karate Chop.

4.) **While tapping the Gamut point on the back of hand between the knuckle of baby finger and ring finger**

(This point is not always used – remember to keep your head still whilst following the instructions below.)

Close your eyes, open your eyes, look down hard right, look down hard left, look round in a circle one way, round in a circle the other way, hum, count 1-5, hum.

5.) **Repeat points in (3)**

6.) **Scale the problem from 1-10 and repeat all of the above again if necessary**

EFT generates confidence, healthy independence and powerful ways to mobilise your resilience

EFT tapping can be used for some of the ups and downs that can happen in life; here I am focusing it on a lack of confidence as well as developing trust. It is a simple and powerful way to support and inspire our lives. I continue to turn to EFT when I notice a block, some resistance or I feel emotionally vulnerable. EFT shines a light on our path to help us to be more at one with ourselves and to release reactions that are not helpful.

---

[2] In some Asian countries this is an aggressive image and for this reason this point is sometimes called "Side of the Hand." In this book we retain the term "Karate Chop Point."

EFT helps a client with her lack of confidence

In my first appointment with Gail, we discussed how she felt about her up-coming interview before we started the EFT tapping. She said her throat already felt tight when she just thought about it.

(Step 1) I asked her how intense from 0-10 (scaling the problem) her throat felt now. She said it was dry and tense – at about a 6.

(Step 2) We tapped together (and Gail followed me through all of the steps) on her karate chop point three times and she said "Even though my throat is tight and dry just thinking of my interview, I deeply and completely respect myself anyway." (the reminder phrase)

(Step 3) We continued tapping 7 times on each of the points and she said "My throat feels dry and tight." (the reminder phrase: a reduced version)

(Step 4) I asked her to tap on her Gamut point whilst just thinking of how she felt and to follow the instructions of moving her eyes, then humming and counting. (Step 5) We repeated Step 3 on all of the points.

(Step 6) I then asked her to notice how dry and tense her throat was (scaling her problem again).

She said it felt a lot better: possibly a 2, but she thought it might go up again before her interview. I suggested that she repeat the EFT procedure to help herself as often as she felt she needed to.

We decided to run through the tapping again to give her additional practice. We began at Step 2 as above with slightly different wording which reflected her concern that it might go up.

(Step 2) I inquired again to find out how she was feeling and she said it was still a 2. I asked her to tap on her karate chop point and say the following reminder phrase three times, "Even though it's a 2 now and I think it could go up again before my interview, I deeply and completely accept myself for thinking this anyway."

(Step 3) After checking in to find out if she still felt the same feelings, she said, "Now that I'm doing it again I feel more confident about practicing this leading up to my interview."

(Step 4) I asked her to think about her last comments as she tapped on her Gamut point and to keep her head still whilst she followed my instructions.

(Step 5) I asked her how she felt after completing this second round, and she shared a new reminder phrase which was "I am much more confident about my interview." She repeated Step 3 using this new reminder phrase.

(Step 6) After completing this second round of EFT I ask Gail to let me know how she was feeling. She said "I feel completely clear now and look forward to my interview." (She scaled her problem as clear.)

Three weeks later Gail rang to let me know she had been offered the job and felt really confident about beginning it in another two weeks.

The real benefit of EFT is its ability to stretch and open us up fully to discover what is actually holding us back or where we may have been hurt in the past. Many time's these painful events are lost in the mists of time; however when tapping on our expressed feelings, vague or not so vague, we can start to find out where the roots of our fears and distress are. Clients say they notice unexpected insights and awareness of how to develop their potential abilities whilst using EFT. It also whets their appetite for understanding and knowing more of who they really are.

We get to know that we matter, that we are enough by clearing the disruption in our energy system, and that we want to let go of a lack of confidence or want to develop trust whilst we are tapping on the EFT acupoints. At the same time we have the opportunity to listen to what is surfacing, how we are feeling, and our body awareness. Our desire to pay attention, to take time to listen deep inside helps us to find our true selves. The cause of all negative emotion is a disruption in our body's energy system. This may have been a trauma, unkind words, or being ignored by someone. Whatever it is, it is held within us.

On some days, we may consider seeking help from a therapist. This could occur when you become aware that you are too close to your problem. An EFT therapist would certainly help with clarity and experience, as they have more emotional distance than we do whilst working on ourselves. Enjoying the opportunity of having a supportive guide helps, inspires and enlivens us to explore the hidden depths of our inner world of desired intentions.

EFT and working with your journal

I invite you now to look back again to the front of your journal with kind and thoughtful appraisal. Whilst rereading your aspirations, ask, "Have I missed a hidden gem of a viable way forward?"

When reading what you have written, ask, "How are these journal words affecting me now?" Then consider ways to do EFT. Be patient if just starting out. EFT is a very forgiving process and even if steps are missed, it works. If ever you are lost for words, just noticing how you are inside will be quite enough.

Possible tapping thoughts for you

Do your earlier aspirations now appear to be way beyond your capabilities? When you first wrote one of your desired intentions in the front of your journal, did you notice that there were submerged fears? If so, where do you feel these? When did you feel them? And to continue our exploration: was there something that could have contributed to your holding back? Or was there someone who perhaps extinguished your light? Now, are you aware of some feelings (you can check your

SUDs level) or maybe resistance? If so, recognising these paves the way for you to clear them. You can do the tapping now, and focus on what may be holding you back. Your emotional intentions connect you to your EFT tapping results.

Keep tapping as you notice changes happening

If you are connecting to your inner world, pay close attention to anything that is coming to you – however simple. And tap on it!

Tapping habitually ensures you benefits. Be loving and patient with yourself as you would be with a little five-year-old. Gary chatters to clients while they both tap together – he calls this "garbage and gold." He explains that there's lots of garbage in what he says as he's talking away; and all the while he is chatting, he is watching, and noticing changes. Then he comes up with the **GOLD** *(he knows it's gold for his client too because of their reactions)*. You too can do this by just talking and tapping on yourself and intently paying attention to what is going on inside of you. Whether you verbalise your thoughts or just notice feelings, simply keep tapping with open awareness. Tap as long as you wish and be with yourself, and hold onto any desires or needs.

Clients say if they end up in confusion, unsure of what to do, tapping at that exact moment helps enormously. That's because EFT settles the disruption in our energy system. As EFT settles this, it can be like a breath of fresh air blowing away our cobwebs. Then, when an inspiring focus comes to you, tapping in your creative desires brings massive shifts to your life. Write these milestones in the front of your journal to support yourself, for future inspiration, confidence and lifting your levels of trust.

At anytime whilst tapping when you wish for a break, go and write up your experiences in your journal. When you record benefits or an opening up of yourself in the front of your journal, this enhances trust in you and your choices. Use your journal almost like it's a person you trust and respect – it will deepen understanding that clears your mind. Trusting yourself so openly in this way builds more confidence in this practice.

I have in the past missed many opportunities to tap when I was feeling angry or frustrated. Now, I absolutely know those are the very best moments for us to do EFT. In Part Three of this book, (I mention simple unobvious ways to do this when you are not alone.) Whenever we are concerned or feel stuck, doing the tapping will be freeing us. Friends say that whatever has been happening inside dramatically changes after they do EFT; they also say that it has opened up unexpected revelations.

Even now, though, I sometimes forget to use EFT and clients tell me that they do too. This happens even after we have enjoyed marvellous breakthroughs. I've found it's because we tend to forget we even had those problems or there are still some subconscious fears or resistance. But, like a good friend, EFT is always with us, waiting and ready to help. EFT is right at our fingertips.

When we have already worked on a specific problem or experience we can use EFT to delve even deeper into it. If it is an old issue, having an open-hearted response facilitates additional healing. So, if you find yourself frustrated by an apparent lack of freedom or progress, be willing to suspend judgement, and as you tap, voice your disappointment, express your frustration. The energy of these negative emotions carries you through the process to positive conclusions. We now know that both positive and negative energies will enhance the flow of energy therapies.

Simple ways to use EFT on yourself

All of the EFT points to tap on are in easily accessible places. They are located on the top of your head your face, your upper body and your hands. You can tap on either side of your body, and if you forget or miss a point, love and forgive yourself anyway!

After they learn EFT, many of our clients share it with family and friends with good results. This means that children, with a little guidance are also helping themselves. Tam and I taught this technique to our children and they in turn shared it with their own children. One day, when our youngest grandson, nearly one, was sitting on my knee, he started coughing. Immediately, his older brother, around two and a half, ran up to him and started tapping on his face. Whilst he tapped on his little brother's face he said, "Bugs, bugs, go away." None of us had even thought of doing this. And it worked! A few months later, as a result of the training I had done with a group of primary school teachers, I was told that their pupils were using EFT as naturally as any other routine behaviour.

If you watch Youtube or videos of various other therapists working with EFT, you may notice that the routine can vary slightly from one practitioner to another. Just as there are varied schools of acupuncture, there are varied schools of EFT. They each provide support and help.

A number of clients find they don't naturally go to EFT for help, especially in the early days of learning about it. I remember this happened to me very soon after I learnt it. I had been struggling because Gary had asked me to write a case history for his website. I found myself getting upset because writing a client case history reminded me of how upset I had felt at school. Tam asked, "Why don't you tap on it?" and I said no. Looking back on this now, one of the reasons I didn't was because I thought it was too trivial a problem for me to tap on. And at the same time, I remember thinking that I ought to just do it and see if it could actually help me, but my logical mind said, "Oh, this is such old stuff: it's too late to do anything about it!" And I listened to that part of me.

Tam was right – I did need to tap on it. Honouring your feelings is a truly beautiful and loving way to treat your fears. Anyone of us can have this resistance as I did – it's a feeling of 'For goodness sake, pull yourself together! What's the matter with you?' At times our self-criticism can be very cruel. But we now have a choice and EFT tapping will and can move us past this habit. And we can choose to move towards experiencing self-love.

I therefore encourage clients and students to tap on any experiences that could be disrupting their energy system. Gary talks about the disruption in our body system as being almost like electrical static: the zzzzzt that affects our system when we are in disharmony within. EFT works so effectively as we tune into our physical pain, strong feelings, and powerful emotions. Oftentimes physical pain is related to the emotional component of the injury, where we can be blaming ourselves for getting hurt, worrying about why we are slow to recover as well as taking on board the diagnosis given to us by a professional. All these are challenges that are very amenable to tapping with far-reaching results.

When clients feel under a lot of pressure to perform, their stress levels can be high. The stress response in many high-powered professional positions can be effectively alleviated with EFT. These clients report that their sleep, digestion and health are far more stable. This also applies to high-profile sports personnel when they want to perform and to be at their very best. They confirm that EFT often releases fears and reduces the pressure they have piled on themselves. They are then able to perform at their optimum level and are no longer hampered by their negative programming.

We now know that tapping on ourselves compassionately enables us to neutralise painful memories and experiences that may in the past have hijacked our success. Opening our heart to these gives us very real ways to reassure and re-educate the subconscious part of our brain. Our positive expectancy, being there for ourselves and using energy psychology routines such as EFT can switch off our outdated fight and flight mechanisms. Now, our unconditional love will open the way to our true freedom.

Using EFT to release disappointment when it is just not working

It is understandable that we experience disappointment when EFT is working well for others but not for us. However, when we voice this frustration, expressing exactly how we feel, EFT will frequently and surprisingly lead the way to a major breakthrough. The intensity of how we feel connects us to the problem and clears away the trauma or disruption in our body's energy system. Passively tapping without any emotional connection rarely helps because we are not connected to, or in tune with, any feelings or thoughts.

Practitioners and those who simply share EFT with others can find that they help others with success, and then they very occasionally discover they are not obtaining as favourable results from using EFT on themselves. One possible reason is that they are so used to doing it on others, that, as carers, they are taking a back seat in their own lives. And it is also true that it is sometimes easier to work on someone else, as we can be less involved and more objective. When this disappointment occurs, it is important to get ourselves out of our own way and be persistently determined in working through this with EFT. We can feel sadness, frustration, disappointment or even anger and then put pressure on ourselves with phrases like "Why doesn't it work as well for me! I can help others – what's the matter with me?" Using this type of EFT chatter whilst tapping and connecting to how we feel about it will, with our desire and persistence, move us out of that space and into a genuine connection to our needs.

An experienced therapist was training a group, and as part of the training, he often demonstrated on individual members of the group. He asked a number of people from the audience to come up onto the stage if they were currently experiencing pain (they had had medical checks) and would be willing to use EFT. Ten attendees lined up, and were asked by the trainer to describe their pain/stiffness, and the SUDs level of pain they were experiencing.

After this, the trainer asked them and everyone who wanted to in the audience to follow him through some tapping using their own descriptive words. Following one or two rounds of EFT, those who were on the stage were asked to measure their SUDs level again. Two or three out of the ten reported that they no longer had any discomfort. They were then asked to check again by noticing if this was still the case after they gently moved their bodies. Those who were happy with their results left the stage and went back to their seats.

The rest, including any in the audience who were tapping along, continued to do EFT until a more comfortable state was achieved. This left only one attendee still on the stage. He had gout and he said it was maybe a little better, so he left the stage and sat down. At the end of the day, the trainer suggested to him that it would be helpful if he continued to tap on himself for the pain whilst he was at home. The following morning, just as the training was about to begin, this attendee ran down the lecture theatre and up onto the stage. He then proceeded to dance an Irish jig, and at the same time declared that he was now pain-free.

After the training weekend and his experiences with gout, this same trainer continued to help many others who came to him with gout. These new clients also received surprisingly positive results. Then, strangely enough, sometime later, he himself developed gout – he had never had it before. However, it did not worry him because he knew that he could help himself using EFT, which he did. The gout went away when he tapped, but then it came back. So, he did EFT again, it went away again and then came back. This happened a number of times and it began to frustrate him. The next time he tapped, these were the words he used: "Even though I can help other people, but I cannot help myself, I deeply and completely respect myself anyway." He repeated this louder and stamped his foot because he was frustrated that it kept coming back and it was painful to walk. The energy of his frustration and the EFT tapping did the trick, because even now, many years later, gout has never come back in any way, shape or form.

EFT benefits after working through an early school trauma

A young man called Kevin came to my clinic with serious stress issues. He worked in a special needs unit that he loved. For the past six weeks he had been experiencing severe panic attacks which were waking him at night. Whilst thinking about his nightmares, he said his level of anxiety was a SUDs level of 8, and he described his discomfort as a twisting in his stomach.

As we began to tap around the points, he told me how he was feeling. His description was "I feel I'm going to die at night and I really want to live. The children I care for need me to help them. I deeply respect myself anyway." We continued around all his face points, his collarbone and under his arm. I asked him how he was feeling and he said his fear was much better. Then he said, "I can now see my manager's angry face shouting at me." He said she was not explaining why she was angry (and in fact she never did). For a long time she had been openly belittling him.

We started his second round of tapping, starting on his karate chop point again. This time he said, "I don't understand, all I want is to help these little ones, so I completely love and respect my desires to help anyway." As he continued tapping, he became very upset and said, "I feel just like I did when I was little at school, being told off by my very first teacher, and I don't know why." So now his reminder phrase was "I feel like I'm little me at school again."

His next two rounds were used to reduce the intensity of this early trauma. When he started tapping, he said, "She's telling me off again and I don't know why – why's she doing this to me? – I'm so scared of her and all the children are laughing at me – there's nobody there to help me – What if doing this now can help me completely – what a difference this could make to my life! I'm willing to do this tapping for little me, whenever I need to, to let this go – I deserve better than this – I did then and I do right now." When he settled down, he was calmer, so I suggested that he could relax with his easy natural breathing rhythm.

He never knew why this teacher was so critical of him. Even when his parents visited the school to discuss this with the head teacher, no feedback was forthcoming. His father found a new job in another area soon after this event. This family move naturally settled him into a new school, where he was very happy; his concerns had never re-surfaced again until now with his current position and this very critical manager.

As he discussed all of these experiences with me, I asked him to gently continue to press on his finger and thumb points himself whilst he talked and I showed him how he could just squeeze the sides of his fingers and thumb with his other hand whilst off-loading all of these traumas. (This technique is part of SET, another energy psychology therapy. It has its own section later on in the book.) Doing this insured that he would be clearing whilst he was telling me his story about what had been happening in his life.

At this point, I suggested that we use the biofeedback monitor. He was very interested to do this. His levels were showing just how calm he was now. Later, still on the machine, I asked him what he was thinking about as he relaxed, and a smile lit up his face as he told me he was seriously considering looking for a more caring and more congenial place to work. His calm and more relaxed state continued to be the case even when he recalled the events we had explored during EFT. Even when he talked about his desire to find a more harmonious profession, his level of calm never wavered.

Towards the end of this appointment, Kevin became completely relaxed whilst we created his personal self-hypnosis CD recording to take home. When he came again, two weeks later, he had already enjoyed two interesting job interviews. One month later, he sent me an email to let me know that he had found a new position and that he was very happy.

Clearing an intense fear of the dentist with EFT

This client rang because she wanted help to go to the dentist. Her daughter Debbie was to be married and Jenni felt self-conscious about her teeth. In the first part of our appointment, she discussed with me the fact that she had experienced many traumatic dental treatments early in life and had since then avoided going to the dentist. We worked through one upsetting experience where the nurse was instructed to hold her down whilst the dentist did whatever he had to do to her. Jenni's mother was present throughout these proceedings and her comments to Jenni were very critical.

At the end of our appointment, she felt much more confident about going for treatment. I recommended a lovely lady dentist who helped, and continues to help, many of my clients. This dentist first meets anxious clients for a coffee and chat away from the surgery and only proceeds to the surgery and treatment after building their confidence and trust. She also plays them their pre-recorded CDs that I have made if they wish. Jenni rang before the second session of her appointment to cancel it, and to let me know that her dental treatment had gone well and she was very happy with herself.

Two or three years later, Jenni rang me in a very distressed state and asked to make an appointment as soon as possible. I was able to make her appointment very quickly. When she arrived, she told me that she was having flashbacks, insomnia and panic attacks. Her daughter Debbie was expecting a baby in three or four months and since she had become pregnant, Jenni had been waking up in a sweat from nightmares. She knew why she felt frightened: Debbie's pregnancy reminded her of the two very traumatic births she herself had experienced.

(On both occasions she had haemorrhaged badly and was sure she was going to die. Fortunately for Jenni, her father-in-law had been able to arrange and pay for a specialist to be available for both births. Understandably now, she was worried that her daughter could have similar complications, although she had been reassured that this was not at all likely to happen.)

Jenni really wanted to be happy and supportive of her daughter and to enjoy her grandchild, and these early traumas were affecting her happiness. She also did not want to transmit her fears to her daughter. During this appointment we did a lot of EFT to unearth and neutralise an extremely traumatic experience that Jenni had had as a tiny little girl playing in the backyard at her home. She saw a worker fall from a ladder and die as a result of the fall. During this horrific experience, little attention was given to Jenni and her distress – nor was much attention paid to the workman. There was more concern with the problem of insurance coverage for this accident than for what had actually happened.

I made another appointment with Jenni for two weeks later and asked her to ring if she needed an earlier time and to let me know how she was sleeping and feeling. Within two or three days, she rang to say she was sleeping well, was so much more relaxed and happily looking forward to enjoying the arrival of her grandchild. Jenni never needed a further appointment after clearing this very early trauma.

After reading this case history, would you too like to support yourself through an experience using EFT? Do help yourself and use EFT tapping if your feelings about your difficulty are not too strong. When we have big traumas, it is wise to have the support of an experienced EFT practitioner to help us work through the intensity of our distress. However, if you know that something has happened to you previously and it still bothers you, and if you feel confident whilst using EFT on yourself, the following exercise will help you.

EFT journal tapping exercise

In the back of your journal write down some of the details you remember of something that has upset you. While you are writing and you notice emotional or physical symptoms, put your pen down and begin to tap your karate chop point. Express your discomfort in your set-up statement and note the SUDs level and where the feelings are inside. Then, as you begin to relax, pick up your pen again and write whatever you want to remember whilst it is still fresh for you. Re-check the SUDs level and think of what you had been tapping on again whilst you scan your body and mind for any indicators of just how it actually feels now. When all is well, write some positive words or experiences in the front of your journal. These may well have come to you during this time of tapping. At night-time, for example, as you are drifting off to sleep, you can recall them. Doing this will reconnect you to times of fulfilment or achievement or remembering how you felt after clearing this disruption with EFT. Write your thoughts in the front of your journal as soon as you recall them in the morning so that they inspire you when you need them.

An introduction to Pat Carrington's Choices Method

Dr Pat Carrington developed the Choices Method (see *References* for details for her website and books) that can be used to help our lack of confidence or our dependence on others. After Pat used EFT with clients and cleared their blocks and fears to moving forward, she then asked them what their choices would be for their lives. I watched one of Pat's videos, which illustrated how the Choices Method unfolds. I describe it below.

Working with a snake phobia

Pat's female client had many bad memories that were related to snake experiences in her life. Pat worked with a specific memory the client had of being out in the country, and watching her little daughter toddle towards her. As she continued to watch her little one come closer, she saw that a snake was very near to her daughter. Pat picked up on this part of the story to do EFT on this client.

The mother was encouraged to say what she felt and here are her words:

"Even though I was sickened to death, no wonder I was terrified for her life."

After saying this and similar words for some time and reducing the intensity of this terrible experience, Pat asked her to use a choice for the next part of her EFT process. Here is the choice she used:

"Even though I was sickened to death, I choose to remember how perfectly she survived."

This phrase was continued for a whole round of tapping on all of the points. The Choices Method completely changed this mother's state of being and completely released the impact of this trauma. In her thoughts, there was no longer harm or hurt, so she could celebrate and let go completely – she held in her heart how perfectly her little girl survived instead of thinking about a possible disaster.

I have noticed that using the Choices Method is a beautiful and very effective way to complete healing and allow the user to move on freely.

Little Tom's story ends successfully with the Choices Method

Tom, as a little boy, became very frightened when he was playing with friends in a field of hay bales. One bale collapsed and enveloped him with dust and bits that badly affected his breathing. He was quickly rushed to a local village doctor who kindly reassured him, calmed him and let him go back to the holiday camp with his mother.

It was many years later on a trip home from a business conference in Spain that his breathing fears surfaced again. Tom's plane was grounded with suspected technical problems and the passengers were not allowed to disembark. As they waited on the tarmac in the heat without any air conditioning, Tom became deeply distressed and struggled to breathe. The cabin crew asked him if he had his asthma inhaler handy. As he had never had asthma he was puzzled by their question. On his return home, he visited his doctor and shared what had happened on the plane. Tom was referred to me by a consultant from the local hospital for some hypnosis. However whilst using hypnosis, I hit a brick wall. So I introduced EFT to him instead.

SUDs level 8 - Tom started tapping on his karate chop point, and his set-up statement was: "Even though I have this tightness in my chest, I completely respect myself anyway." Before the next round he noticed the tightness wasn't as strong and now he noticed that it was heavy.

SUDs level 6 - Tom's reminder phrase as he tapped on his face, body and hands was "This heavy weight on my chest." As he did this, I noticed his breathing became calmer. Whilst he was still tapping, I said to him, "What does this heavy weight remind you of?" He described to me in detail the frightening moment when the hay bale fell on him. As he described this, he continued to follow me by tapping on himself for three more rounds.

Because Tom still showed signs of distress, I started to continuously tap on the Nine Gamut point at the back of his hand and guided him through the Gamut point procedure. (See Step 4 in the EFT process.)

After this, Tom's reactions were calmer, however I felt that spending time doing some choices would complete things for him in a more rounded way. So we did the Choices Method.

Tom's Choices: "Even though all of this happened to me as a little boy and more recently in Spain, I choose to remind myself it was the heat, the hay, and not asthma. I choose to remember that that kind doctor's words were right for me then, and they are right for me now." After tapping in these choices for three rounds, he said he felt confident to do tapping again if he ever needed to because he knew that the heat was the link that triggered his hay incident to his hot plane panic feelings on the tarmac. This insight made all the difference to his renewed confidence in himself – and he also knew that he had healthy lungs.

Dr Pat Carrington's website: http://patcarrington.com
Journal choices reflection exercise

Incorporating the Choices Method into your Journal Work

Give yourself some time to look through the back section of your journal. Reflect on some events that you offloaded there. Now, ask yourself, "How do I feel today as I revisit this?" "Will this feeling or memory benefit from incorporating the Choices Method?" If the answer is yes, do try it out.

Chapter Six: A Brief Summary

In this chapter, you were introduced to:
The EFT routine
The benefits from EFT
The Choices Method

CHAPTER SEVEN

Tapas Acupressure Technique (TAT)

A number of Gary Craig's early videos contained brief introductions to other energy psychology-based therapies. These were filmed when there were breaks during Gary's EFT seminars. One of the therapies I watched was TAT (Tapas Acupressure Technique). Tapas Fleming, a licensed acupuncturist, developed the TAT technique after visualizing a new way to help others whilst resting in between clients. Tapas began using gentle touch to specific acupoints with her clients, and she observed that this way of working was achieving better results than her current acupuncture treatment.

As Tam and I watched Tapas on Gary's video, we fell in love with her – she is loving, warm, and intuitive. Her approach is very effective. We were so impressed with what she did that we decided to show the videos to our EFT students. When they saw Tapas in action they realised that here was another interesting way to support our growth and free us from trauma using energy psychology.

During the 2000 ACEP Energy Psychology Conference in Las Vegas, both Gary and Tapas were there in person. I worked and learned from both. During my training with Tapas, I experienced the TAT benefits for my own problems. Tam also experienced healing shifts. This meditative technique uses two fingers and the thumb of one hand with the lightest touch to points on the face and at the same time the other hand is placed to support the back of the head. This is used for the TAT treatment and is called the TAT pose. Whilst in the pose there is no pressure on the three face points.

I illustrate the TAT pose for you below.

The thumb pad and ring finger pad rest lightly in the corners of your eyes along each side of your nose whilst your middle finger rests on your third eye. At the same time, your left hand supports and cups the back of your head.

The Seven Steps of TAT

Before each step, take the pose, and after each step take your hands down.

Step 1
Put your attention on the problem.
When you have felt a shift, ask yourself:
"What happened?"

Step 2

Put your attention on the opposite condition.

"What happened?"

Step 3

Say this out loud or in your mind: "All the origins of this problem are healing now."

"What happened?"

Step 4

Say out loud or in your mind one of the following statements: whichever resonates with you.

"All of the places in my mind, body and life where this has / been a problem/resonated/ been held/been stuck / are healing now."

or

"God, thank you for healing all the places in my mind, body and life where this has / been a problem /resonated/been held/been stuck."

"What happened?"

Step 5

Say either of these two statements:

"All the parts of me that got something out of having this problem are healing now."

or

"God, thank you for healing all the parts of me that got something out of having this problem."

"What happened?"

Step 6

"I forgive everyone I blamed for this problem, including God, (another person) and myself."

"What happened?"

Step 7

"I ask forgiveness of everyone I hurt because of this problem."

"What happened?"

During a TAT treatment with a therapist, clients take up the TAT pose. Whilst in the pose, they put their attention on what they want help or guidance with. They become very present in the pose position and silently allow their thoughts to wander around their problem. Then, when a shift in focus is felt, they take both hands down and talk to their therapist about what happened whilst they did TAT. Therapists who practice TAT are very present with their clients – they look at them and listen with an open heart to whatever they have to say. After this step, when the clients have shared what happened and are ready to continue, they take up the TAT pose again and put their attention onto the next step of the TAT process.

A client uses TAT on herself

After I familiarised one of my clients with TAT, she went home and used it on herself. She wanted to find out why she refused to eat certain foods.

Since childhood, this client would intentionally avoid numerous foods although she had no physical reaction to them; it was just an avoidance – there were no allergies.

In step one she took up the pose and allowed her mind to wander around in a state of listening openness for one to two minutes on the problems she experienced for certain foods. *When she took her hands down, she wrote down in her journal some of these thoughts that came into her mind.*

In step two she took up the pose again and allowed her mind to wander around the opposite condition to this problem. This was of enjoying eating some of the things she had been avoiding up until that point. *She wrote in her journal that she could choose to eat anything that she would like to try from now on and be happy with new tastes of other foods.*

In step three she took up the pose again and allowed herself to wander around the origins of her problem. *She realised in that moment that the origins of her problem had begun at school when she was unable to choose what she ate for her dinner each day at lunchtime and it was a struggle for her. She acknowledged this in the back of her journal.*

In step four she took up the pose and let herself be with the people that she had subconsciously blamed for her problem. *As she thought about the dinner ladies that she blamed for her problem, she realised they may not have had any choice. There was a shift in her perception and she found herself forgiving them for what they were expected to serve up to the children and she also forgave herself for blaming them. These notes on forgiveness of others and of herself were entered in her journal too.*

This client did only these TAT steps spontaneously when she left the training; this worked well for her at the time. Later in this chapter we consider a one-step procedure. Much of TAT is about following how we are feeling.

A week later this client rang me to say that she was now enjoying carrots as well as custard and was eager to try other foods she had been refusing. Her block seemed to have been resistance to trying foods. Now she felt free to choose anything she wished to, and if she didn't like it she could leave it or throw it away. Some weeks later in a new restaurant, she happily tried all of the food on her plate and was also happy with leaving some when she had enjoyed it enough. She recalled that in the past she had felt strong resistance when there were suggestions of eating out – she had been happy going to only one particular restaurant and had avoided others.

Her previously intense reactions had caused disharmony with family and friends on many occasions. However, when she told them about this strong resistance, they were very kind and understanding. The last time I heard from her, she told me her eating resistances had cleared and that now, she always looked forward to eating out.

Using TAT

At one training with Tapas, a woman participant kept going into the pose position in coffee breaks and whenever else she could; she eventually ended up feeling poorly with a splitting headache. Tapas said to her, "You will not do any more TAT today and in future whenever you use TAT you must limit it to no more than twenty minutes a day." This recommendation applies to us all. As it is a deeply calming and meditative experience, often we want more time than this because it releases so much stuck energy and tension. However, it's not good for us to overdose on TAT!!

Welcome TAT and simply let go

Tapas says people have asked her over the years how to figure out what to work on with yourself or a client. Since we can each present huge amounts of material, we need to consider what would be best to address. First of all: don't worry. Tapas encourages her clients to allow themselves to wander around their problem while they sit in the pose position. The description Tapas uses for this is "When we grasp and haul in a piece of a net, it makes no difference which corner we are in contact with because it is all connected to the whole, thereby providing healing for whatever is needed."

What's important to know is that thoughts have different types of energy and that at specific moments in our lives we experience specific types of energy. Also, we need to recognise thoughts as things. They are invisible but they do exist. Some thoughts have been with us since we were children. Some are new to us and give us courage and happiness. Other thoughts that are not so happy repeat over and over and keep us from realising our dreams. Some pop up in certain situations; others are a constant, low-level drone. Thoughts have a great influence on the flow of our lives.

TAT is a powerful tool which helps us to follow our dreams as well as release negative thoughts that come to mind. When we take the TAT pose we can choose to work with either of these intentions.

Watching Tapas in action with a client was inspirational. During a TAT treatment there were distinct signs of their letting go. At the end of their treatment, their faces shone and they were alight with joy. On completion of a TAT treatment, Tapas often looked at the audience and said, "Just take a look at their face."

For information on the latest up-to-date TAT procedure please visit Tapas Fleming's site. www.TatLife.Net and happier now with a taste of TAT® in our FREE three-part v.

TAT and the Art of Practising Presence

Tam and I studied with Tapas over a number of years after 2000. When using this technique for myself as well as with my clients I have observed how meditative it is. It is remarkable in that as a TAT practitioner, I am totally present, intently observing my client, and I listen deeply when my clients report their experience after each step of the procedure. (This presence is particularly remarkable compared to other therapies where I would usually be more proactive.) Tapas calls this deep listening "practicing presence."

Letting the process flow without my words or intervention while just being there and getting myself out of the way is what is meant to happen. My client and I are open to whatever happens and throughout this, their healing unfolds. The space for healing is held until it is revealed. This energy therapy technique of just allowing my client time to be with whatever is happening throughout their therapy sessions brings wonderful breakthroughs. It benefits me as the therapist: I am present and listening and witnessing deeply; it benefits the clients because they feel safe and truly heard.

Tapas Fleming's own personal One-Step TAT Process

Tapas came to the UK a number of times and stayed with us in South Yorkshire. On one of her visits, she shared with me the following one-step procedure. I have shared this with clients and friends, and I often use it now, years later, for myself. At the time that she gave it to me, she said that she had found it helpful for herself whenever she was pressed for time. It's simple and only takes a few moments out of your day and it certainly clears the way towards a calmer state of being. I find this is the case, whatever is going on in my life. Enjoy making time for this as a gentle loving moment to be present with yourself.

The One-Step

Whenever you notice a problem or find that something is troubling you, take a little time before taking up the pose to be present with whatever it is that is troubling you – there is no need to express it, only to notice it. Then after this gentle awareness of your problem, take up the TAT pose and allow your mind to wander around the opposite condition to the problem. What you are doing, then, is focusing on what you desire instead of the problem. Do this until a shift happens. This could be for one or two moments, or if you hold the pose for longer, you might notice after a while that you are no longer engaged with what had been troubling you. When a change has occurred, take your hands down and acknowledge with gratitude how good being present with yourself is for you.

Whilst I am sharing this one-step procedure with you now, I have not seen it featured on Tapas's website or in her training material. However, I believe it is a simple way to be present with intention and centred in the here and now. The experience of doing TAT is often so meditative that some clients are tempted to stay in the pose or to take up the pose more than once in a day. However, do remember that caveat mentioned earlier: Tapas recommends spending no more than <u>twenty</u> minutes in any one day in the TAT therapy pose. She also suggests that you drink plenty of water whilst working with this energy therapy technique.

Journal Reflection Point:

Your TAT One-Step procedure reflection for yourself

Have you tried the one-step procedure? Did you jot down some points that you felt? And how they shifted? What you experience and what you write will most likely be different from one day to another. You can do this one-step procedure as a way to experience more clarity and to give you daily insights.

Tapas Fleming's website: <u>www.tatlife.net</u>

Chapter Seven: A Brief Summary

In this chapter you learnt that:
The TAT pose is the same for each step
The basic procedure has seven steps
Whilst practicing presence shifts happen
TAT treatments are limited to twenty minutes a day
Hydrating during TAT is very important

CHAPTER EIGHT

Muscle Testing And Be Set Free Fast (BSFF)

Larry Nims, like Gary Craig, trained first with Dr Roger Callahan in TFT (Thought Field Therapy) and again like Gary, he simplified the TFT method – in his own unique way. His therapy is usually known by its initials: BSFF (Be Set Free Fast).

Its full descriptive name is Behavioural and Emotional Symptom Elimination Training for Resolving Excess Emotions: Fear, Anger, Sadness, and Trauma. Larry used these words to describe how BSFF can help us all.

Muscle testing and BSFF

Muscle testing gives us feedback from our body of how we are feeling or relating to a situation, a person or an event. It does this by giving an indication of the strength or weakness of the muscle being tested. It is of immense benefit in BSFF, and is usually carried out before and after the treatment. (Later on in the chapter, you will read more about how and when this is used.)

BSFF links you to Finding and Accepting You

Tam and I learnt about Larry on Gary Craig's videos, and subsequently saw him in action at the ACEP conference in 2000. We found this technique to be very interesting and the beneficial results for those who went up on the stage could be seen immediately by their positively strong muscle tests. These results were also obvious because Larry's clients were excited and happy to be free from what he calls "the emotional roots" of their problem.

Tam and I trained with Larry and received his permission to teach others. We have over the years noticed significant success from this simple technique.

Initially, Larry focuses on using muscle testing on the statements that he says to participants which connect specifically to where they are wanting help. Then Larry asks participants to choose their "cue word." Following this, he gives a once-only instruction to their subconscious mind that includes the suggestion that, "Whenever I say or think of my chosen cue word which is ...., you, my subconscious mind, will do the entire BSFF treatment for my problem." The BSFF treatment combines conscious awareness, intention and cueing the subconscious. These, along with the client's intention, eliminate the chronic stress and emotional and physical pain for whatever problem is showing up.

Almost always no tapping is needed. After their chosen cue word is used, the client has a muscle test. The muscle test is used to find out if their problem has cleared or if more work needs to be done. When the muscle test is weak there may still be a hidden underlying issue that needs treatment. When there is, this is checked out with the client using a number of statements, which are muscle tested separately. These statements are connected to the specific issues which each client has been working on.

Over the years, Larry has adjusted the instruction statement to the subconscious mind a number of times. Visiting his website will keep you up to date. (The above suggested one is, however, adequate and still very relevant today.)

How does BSFF work?

BSFF teaches the subconscious mind – through direct communication, learning and expectancy – to follow instructions whilst we use our cue word. The cue eliminates self-defeating emotional responses, including both our psychological and physiological reactions. These problems cause unnecessary pain and problems in our lives. The subconscious responds to our instruction, when we say or think of our cue. It then alerts the subconscious mind to act to eliminate our obsolete conditioned subconscious programme that no longer serves any purpose in our lives.

Larry's intuitive belief is that our subconscious mind is a faithful servant that will respond to our request for help. My own perception of this is that, in our asking we receive. The use of a cue word is linked to our intention in asking for healing. BSFF can be applied any time you want, whether you are out and about, at work, when there are friends or family around...

Here is a simple way to use BSFF

First of all, think of a word you want to use as a cue word: any word will do. Here are two examples of cue words: one friend of mine uses "rats" and my cue word is "peace." Then, when your intended cue has been said out loud to yourself or you have non-verbally registered your cue word, to your subconscious mind: "Whenever I think or say my cue word (use your chosen cue word here) you, my subconscious mind, will do the entire BSFF treatment for me for this problem (you name your problem)." Larry says, "If you forget your cue, you can use another one or even have a number of cues on hand to use."

When you use BSFF, you need to:

1.) Have a desire to be free of a problem
2.) Have a trust in, and a willingness to use, BSFF
3.) Think of asking and receiving
4.) Decide on a cue word

5.) Read or say Larry's instructions out loud

6.) Use your cue word

When Tam and I first learnt about using a cue word instead of tapping on the points, we wondered how this could ever work. We found we were not the only ones to wonder; Larry said he was often asked that question. He said, "Just use your cue word for any of your understandable disbelief too. Keep it simple and say, 'Treat that,' frequently say or think your cue word and ask in this way whenever you need help or notice a problem."

BSFF for confidence and self-image

Larry says that he usually treats self-confidence and self-image as the first two problems with his clients. These impact upon almost every part of life. Treating these first frequently helps to reduce the treatment needed.

Larry states that the subconscious mind will comprehensively treat all self-image/self-confident issues with the following statement:

"I am now treating, in one treatment, **all** of the negative self-image problems, and all negative thoughts, attitudes and feelings that I am now, or have ever been, holding or that I have ever agreed with, about myself." Then say "Treat all of these" and your cue word.

As with all energy therapies or other treatments you receive, you pay attention to how you are afterwards.

A simple BSFF treatment for performance anxiety

Whenever I notice a problem of performance anxiety, I say, ""Whenever I think or say *Peace*, you, my subconscious mind, will do the entire BSFF treatment for me for my public speaking anxiety." I then say, "Treat," and "Peace." Afterward, I test my results with a sway test. If my response is weak, I do BSFF again.

A client uses BSFF

When a client returned to our clinic for her second treatment with me, she asked if she could use BSFF for the frustration she was feeling towards her dog Watson. He was still fairly young and she was currently training him for recall. She said her dog had selective hearing when she called him and this made her angry. She knew her own energy level was affecting him so she wanted help with this reaction. She had chosen **listens** as her cue word. I asked her to think of the BSFF suggestion that whenever she was thinking of this problem and she used her cue word, her subconscious mind would do the treatment for her for this. For a few moments, she stood calmly and thought of this problem whilst using her cue word. Then to test the results, she used the sway test as a muscle test using her words: "Thank you, I am completely free of this negative energy now," and she swayed forward to this statement.

(This muscle test is given in more detail below under the heading of **examples of muscle tests**)

After leaving me, she continued to use **listens** and the words "Treat that" at times when she felt she was becoming stressed with Watson. After a couple of weeks, she was really happy and surprised by the fact that with the help from BSFF her energy levels were much calmer and the volume on her stress levels had been turned down appreciably. These, together with her slower, more measured breathing worked well in helping her and her dog Watson. The benefits for this client were that she was much more confident about her training and her dog was becoming more obedient. He came to her side when she called him much more frequently.

Examples of muscle testing which may be used with BSFF and other applications

Two Self-Help Muscle Tests to Use on Your Own

Muscle testing is a valuable way to connect to your sense of knowing. The result of your muscle test is an indicator from your body giving you feedback on when you are physically, emotionally and spiritually strong or weak. The results are connected to the energy of your beliefs, and the images, feelings, sounds, aromas and tastes and words that you are experiencing within.

Whilst using a muscle test we may use any muscle. These tests can show how aligned we are to our thoughts and to what we are stating. Usually, when we speak our truth we are strong. That's why weight lifters say, "Yes Yes Yes!" when lifting weights.

The Sway Technique

The sway test is easy to do and it doesn't require another person. This test could be used when you are testing the results of BSFF after using your cue. It is one of the simplest methods of obtaining a yes, a neutral or a no response from within. To do this, stand still with your feet hip-width apart. In most circumstances, an instinctive sway forward of your body indicates a move towards whatever you desire. A sway backwards indicates you want to move away from something. Remaining in the upright position may mean that the results are neutral. You could use the sway test in your own home to start with. To do this, think of two possible fruits to choose from for breakfast that you have in your home. A pear or a banana maybe. Then pick up one fruit – the fruit you fancy – and say, "This is good for me," and notice what is happening to your body. Practicing this for a number of statements and scenarios over a few days will help you to become aware of how your body is responding.

If you feel confident doing this at home, then try this in a shop. When, for example, you go to choose a birthday card for a friend, say or think "X (your friend's name) would love this card." Notice if there is movement in your body, forward or backwards. Continue to practise, so that in the future when you want help for a more complex decision you will be confident to accept a message from your body.

Easy Yes and No Responses we often take for granted

If you apply a yes/no response test when looking at your menu, look at your choices in the menu and say or think, "This is good for me." At that moment, you might very possibly notice a slight nod or perhaps a slight shake of your head in response. Frequently, it is more of an intuitive, felt sense inside that you feel. This yes/no response can be used in many situations. Perhaps at times when you are unsure about whether you should make that phone call, buy that present, or send that message. I have found this helpful when choosing titles for my handouts when there is more than one title to choose from. Experiment and see for yourself!

Over time, as you experiment and practise, your felt experiences become even more available to you. Your openness to receive without judgement or resistance makes a huge difference to you accessing the information you need or of just knowing it.

How to set up a muscle test with a friend for your confidence and self-image

Before starting, explain to your friend why muscle tests are helpful.

Then, choose some positive statements for yourself. Here are some examples of muscle test statements to use. These will highlight the areas to work on. If your muscle test is weak it means that the statement is not entirely true.

I like myself
I have a good mind
I deserve a good life
I am a worthwhile person

Ask your friend to stand behind you, so that you will not be looking at one another whilst doing this test. Then, stretch your right arm level with your shoulder out to the side. Then say, "My name is........." Your friend says "Hold," to you before she presses down just above your wrist. Your friend should use the same amount of pressure each time you carry out this muscle test and always say "Hold," before pressing down. Whenever you say a statement that is true for you, you would expect a strong muscle test response (your arm will stay horizontal). If you test with a false statement, the muscle would usually be weak and your arm would descend with the pressure.

To avoid undue stress, as you practise, change arms when it is appropriate.

What you do after this will depend on the strength of your muscle test. If it is strong, you have no need to treat further because the muscle test is showing that you are happy with the positive muscle test statement and result.

If the muscle test is weak, you would do another muscle test with a different statement.

You can do this for your friend too.

An informative arm muscle test

I was muscle-testing a participant using her name, Patricia. To test the strength of her arm muscles on what we would expect to be strong, I asked her to say, "My name is Patricia." I followed the procedure just mentioned above.

As highlighted above, if her arm remained strong, her response would be a positive response to the test. So the fact that her arm tested weak was a big surprise to me. We discussed this in the group afterwards and she said, "Everyone actually calls me 'Pat.' Is that why I was weak?" So her response to Patricia was weak because subconsciously she thought of herself as Pat. Whilst doing a further test on her, I asked her to say, "My name is Pat." This true statement then produced a strong muscle test.

Enjoy discovering more about yourself, your needs, desires and positive intentions and explore simple muscle testing. If it is new to you, do this with an open heart too.

Another informative muscle test

During our energy therapy workshops, we include muscle testing.

Earlier in the day of a workshop, I had overheard one of the participants mentioning that she did not like fish. Whilst Tam was monitoring the training, I had time to wonder whether there was any way we might be able to illustrate this to the group. I looked into my larder and found a tin of tuna and a tin of bamboo shoots. And very nicely, both tins were the same size.

Whilst I was away from everyone in the group, I wrapped each of these tins separately in identical tea towels. I then asked the tester to give one tin to her partner and ask her to say "This is good for me." The same was done for the second tin. One tested strong and the other tested weak. When the tester unwrapped both tins she found her partner had tested weak on the tuna and strong on the bamboo shoots. No one knew that this student was being tested in this way at the time.

Muscle testing gives us a window into how our thoughts can strengthen or weaken our reactions. In some circumstances, a weak muscle test could save our life if we are allergic to fish because our body knows better than we know consciously.

Dr David Hawkins's book *Power vs. Force: The Hidden Determinants of Human Behaviour* illustrates that some ideas are so weakening that just holding them in mind makes test subjects unable to keep their arms up at all. Other concepts are so powerful that when the subjects hold them in mind, it is impossible to force down their arms.

Journal Reflections:

Which part of this chapter resonated well for you? Many people say they love using the muscle test, while some prefer the simplicity of BSFF especially when they can test their benefit straight away with the sway test. What about you – which one do you like? Have you had a go at doing it? Write down your own experience in the front of your journal.

Chapter Eight: A Brief Summary

In this chapter, you learnt about:
BSFF's cue word
Larry Nims's statement to the subconscious
Muscle testing
The sway test
The Yes/No response test

Dr Larry Nims's website address: - www.BeSetFreeFast.com/

https://www.youtube.com/watch?v=ozc54Wgc9x0

PART THREE

CELEBRATING –
Loving Care For You

CHAPTER NINE

Energy Therapy Gifts For Your Life

Energy therapy techniques are like beautiful jewels. They shine a light into our lives from so many different angles. Each technique picks up one facet or more to open up our emerging potential. For this chapter I have chosen six simple-to-use energy therapy techniques for you to enjoy.

SET (Simple Energy Technique)

Dr David Lake and Steve Wells, both from Australia, created what they call SET (Simple Energy Technique). This development originated from EFT and from BSFF.

When David and Steve use SET in their work, they ask clients, as they talk through how they are feeling or disclosing their needs, to tap or press their finger and thumb points. At the end of the appointment, they ask their clients to notice how they feel and to share their experiences. David and Steve have stated that at the end of their sessions, without exception, all clients report that they feel better.

In the case of SET, no EFT style set-up phrase or reminder phrases are used. There is also no need to measure the SUDs level of discomfort at the beginning or at the end.

Here is one of the many areas in which David and Steve have pushed back the boundaries of their exploration to find out what will work cohesively whilst their clients share their distress or when they choose to release an early trauma during their appointments. The huge benefit of this is that users are less likely to become distressed when they are clearing their emotional and their physical pain. David and Steve also report that they are confident and happy to use this technique on themselves personally whilst they tune into their feelings or notice physical or emotional pain.

When we use SET on ourselves it frequently neutralises our lack of confidence and it calms anxiety. It's simple to use at home, at work, and we can use it unobtrusively when we are out and about too.

When using SET on yourself it is far more effective if you are tuned into and noticing where or how you feel your discomfort. There is no interruption – just incorporating continuous tapping on your fingers and thumb of one or both of your hands. This is usually done with the pad of the thumb on each finger. To tap the thumb, curl your index finger around the thumb of the same hand.

Another really simple way of using SET is to squeeze both sides of your fingers and the thumb with your other hand. This can be done very discreetly under your desk or in your lap. Many business and sports personnel are incorporating it in meetings, on the golf course, or when they are presenting. Many people also report that it is very supportive for them when they are waiting for medical results or receiving treatment in hospital. SET can also be used when working through something together with a group or team. As members stimulate their acupoints on fingers and thumb points during the discussion, creativity and enhanced collaboration may well be sparked.

Recently, David and Steve have suggested that using SET regularly even when we have no particular problem in mind can offer toning benefits to our level of wellbeing. It is very possible that frequently doing SET when we walk, travel, and listen to music – in fact during everyday events – can add to our peace with mind and body.

David and Steve also recommend that we use SET to both prepare before an event as well as prevent a possible future difficulty from happening. This is almost like rehearsal prior to any event or action. We know that this makes sense in sport, or for a band performance practice.

During rehearsal, we are able to be aware of where we require help or practice in advance rather than waiting until the event and finding out we needed some additional experience. Any desirable achievement may also be imagined and this can be carried out within our mind and body. Envisaging our performance whilst doing SET is similar to using self-hypnosis. It requires our intention, desire, and expectation – these are all powerful ways to use our imagination, and practising SET develops our confidence and healthy independence at the core of ourselves.

A client uses SET for overwhelmment

I was introduced to Amy first of all by her friend and colleague Jan who was worried about her. They had worked together for over a year and Jan had noticed how Amy's anxiety was becoming more and more difficult for her to handle. On one occasion she had broken down when she was working with her boss. Jan was really kind to Amy and suggested she came to me for some help.

I felt that asking her to talk would be inappropriate and counterproductive at that time. SET was ideal as it is non-invasive, and easy to follow. When she sat down, I showed her how I used SET on myself. It was obvious that Amy was tuned into her problem so this was the best possible time for her to do this on herself.

After ten minutes Amy started to settle down and was able to say what had happened to upset her. She said that she could not talk to anyone about her problem as disclosing it would be too embarrassing. I reassured her that we could successfully use what we were doing together and it could be done in a way in which she would not need to tell me anything. She said she was surprised to feel so much better already and knew if she felt bad again it would be possible for her to use SET confidently on her own without anyone being too aware of it. She said she would contact me again if she needed additional support.

Journal reflection point:

Have you tried SET on yourself? I would love to know if you have enjoyed using it. The simplicity of using this in any setting means it is very user-friendly. If you receive worthwhile results yourself, just jot down a word or two in your journal so that you can remember it later. Or, share it with a friend or colleague that you are close to: Amy ended up doing just that with her boss!

For more detailed information on SET, go to Dr David Lake and Steve Wells' website: www.eftdownunder.

Free Special Report on SET:

You can download a **complimentary special report** (pdf) by Steve Wells and Dr David Lake, which outlines the main techniques and processes of SET. Click on the following link:

Simple Energy Techniques Special Report

Free SET Audio

Download a free audio of Steve and David talking through SET – It explains what it is, how to use it, and how to integrate SET into your daily life.

Touch and Breath (TAB)

Touch and Breathe (TAB), developed by Dr John Diepold around twenty-five years ago, is a beautiful and gentle way of stimulating acupoints. The points touched are in Chapter 6 – the same ones that are used for EFT. When using this technique, each acupoint is gently touched with one or two fingers, and before moving onto the next point, a deep and easy breath (but not too deep and not strained) is taken with the fingers in place. TAB is calming, it gives the user time to pause, and to be present in the moment wherever they are. It is a wonderful partnership with body, breath, and being at home inside. There may be a reminder phrase or an intentional tuning into the problem with this technique. TAB can be used at anytime and anywhere to suit the individual. Dr Diepold likens the benefits received to the antenna effect equivalent to a TV aerial: whilst touching it there is clarity and when you move, you get fuzz. This time of relaxed contact is important – gentle touching activates the whole and this provides a more sustained connective touch on your acupoints. I find it is especially calming for me when I am feeling unsettled. It is also a very kind method to use for yourself when you have a headache. Using TAB at night-time is very meditative, deeply relaxing and peaceful. The silence and calm of this method means there is no disturbance to partners or those around in the same room at the same time.

Journal reflection point:

TAB reflections to write in your journal

Have you found some different ways and times to use TAB? If you have, why not write these additional ways to do TAB in your journal? It may benefit you at some other point in time.

Here is a link for more information regarding Dr John Diepold's TAB approach. These are available from Dr Pat Carrington's website: -

https://patcarrington.com/**touch-and-breath**-tab-method-article/

Nine TAB ways that you and others can use

TAB's gentle touch has been used very sensitively with little ones.
When you are in pain, it's kinder to use TAB.
Friends say TAB's calm touch on the Gamut point and KC at the same time works well.
When sad, TAB's gentle touch on the inner eyebrow point re-assures.
Settle yourself for a peaceful sleep using TAB on your face points.
Use TAB under your desk at work on your finger and thumb points.
To settle your tummy, use TAB on your under-eye point.
When you feel angry, do TAB on your baby finger.
Forgive yourself by using TAB on your index finger point.

Those who have chronic fatigue syndrome say that TAB is one technique that has helped them to relax more. It gives them the chance to let go of some tension and releases some of their pain. Knowing that there is something they can do consistently uplifts their emotional state as well.

These points are illustrated in Chapter 6 on page xx

ENERGY MEDICINE

After figuring out how to direct her own energies to heal herself of multiple sclerosis in her early thirties, Donna Eden has dedicated her life to empowering others to tune into their own subtle, healing energies using Energy Medicine.

Here is how I came to learn about Energy Medicine. A red-coloured book entitled *Energy Medicine* called out to me many years ago when I was looking through a second-hand bookshelf at an antique fair. At that time I had never heard of EFT or any of the other energy psychology methods. I didn't even know why I wanted to buy the book. After looking through Donna's book and practising some of her exercises, I became fascinated. I was intrigued by this introduction to something that felt totally new.

I was thirsty for more and began to explore the Energy Medicine concept. I bought Donna's more up-to-date book called *Energy Medicine for Women*, and since then, her "five-minute routine" has become an integral part of my life. Once you have practised it most days for two or three weeks, it becomes a wonderful energy pick-me-up. It is not just a routine for women's health; rather it is a wonderful way to support any one of us energetically each and every day.

A description of Energy Medicine from Donna's website

"Energy Medicine awakens energies that bring resilience, joy, and enthusiasm to your life – and greater vitality to your body, mind, and spirit! Balancing your energies balances your body's chemistry, regulates your hormones, helps you feel better, and helps you think better. It has been called the self-care and development path of the future, but it empowers you NOW to adapt to the challenges of the 21st century and to thrive within them."

Donna's website address: edenenergymedicine.com

On the site there is a really helpful video called *Donna's Daily Energy Routine* as well as a questionnaire to Find Your Stress Style. The routine is the official version of the "five-minute" one I mentioned above; it's easy to use, it takes only a short time to do each day and the benefits are very noticeable. Discover for yourself the life-enhancing difference Energy Medicine will give to you.

Thought Field Therapy (TFT) – Stimulating and Sedating Algorithms

Anti-Addiction Algorithms

Sedating
- Between Breasts
- Collar Bone
- Under Breast
- Karate Chop
- Gamut
- Between Breasts

Stimulating
- Under Eye
- Eyebrow
- Under Arm
- Third Eye
- Crown of Head

TFT had its origin in 1979 when Dr Callahan first discovered the problem and treatment of psychological reversal (a way to eliminate self-sabotage and negative thoughts). The following year resulted in the first successful treatment of one of his clients, Mary, who suffered from a very intense phobia of water. You can read a number of accounts of Mary's water phobia story by googling "Dr Roger Callahan's Thought Field Therapy treatment for Mary's water phobia."

Following his success with Mary after he stimulated her under the eye point, which is connected to the stomach meridian point, Dr

Callahan developed Thought Field Therapy (TFT) and came up with what he called an algorithm: a series of small steps in a set order to achieve an intended goal. (A bit like making a pot of tea!) These were specifically researched points to tap on for a range of different problems.

Over a period of time, he created a large number of algorithms, each specifically designed to treat a particular problem; he incorporated them into a very large book that his trained therapists could use on clients' individual needs.

The following two algorithms (out of many others) come from Dr Callahan's TFT work. They are often used for help with addictive cravings. However, there are a lot of other ways we can benefit from including these into our lives. The tapping is carried out in the order illustrated in the diagrams below.

Using the algorithm

A client – a journalist – was using amphetamines to stimulate himself when he wanted more focus in his writing. Then, at the end of the day, when he wished to chill out, he would relax using alcohol. Both of these methods were increasingly detrimental to his health, which is why he came for help. We made a self-hypnosis CD on his intention for healthy ways to achieve his objectives. I introduced him to some EFT tapping at the end of his appointment and also taught him how he could use the stimulating and sedating algorithms to support himself. They both worked well for him and allowed him to be free of his need for the amphetamines and dramatically reduced his alcohol consumption.

I suggested that the stimulating algorithm would be most helpful when he felt he needed a boost of energy before he sat down to do his writing. He tried this out at these times and also found it was helpful if he felt sleepy after his lunch. He knew that doing this was so much better for his health.

Towards the end of his day, replacing his cravings for alcohol with the sedating algorithm reduced the amount (as well as the cost) of his drinking alcohol. Feeling more relaxed helped him to let go in the evening and he emailed me to say he was sleeping like a baby some weeks later. Knowing that it was so much better for the health of his mind and body also added to his self-confidence and general improved wellbeing. Six months after his last appointment I received a card to say that he had lost weight, and felt more energetic. Interestingly, neither intention had been a conscious goal for him.

In the last fifteen years, these two algorithms have helped students, friends and myself in a variety of ways. One student reported that when he sat down to study he felt a loss of energy and momentum. However, after using the stimulating algorithm, he became aware that it cleared his mind as well as energized his body.

A friend told me that she often woke up throughout the night and was unable to get back to sleep. However, after using the sedating algorithm, she was able to drift off again. She continued to do this and found that over a period of two weeks her sleep was rarely disturbed. The only downside to these changes was that she needed to set her alarm – otherwise she found she woke up late. This was a totally new experience for her.

There are many ways to include this in your life. Sometimes we find ourselves rushing around and a little scattered. This could be because something is triggering us subconsciously. When we gently and intentionally take a moment to apply the sedating algorithm, this often settles our stress response simply and easily.

Both algorithms harmonise self-confidence and a healthy, independent balance for a client

A client, Jane, came to me with concerns regarding the fears she often felt when she presented her new project's feasibility to her boss for his feedback before she gave the presentation to the board of directors. Unfortunately, the facial reactions of her boss often affected how she felt afterwards. The facial and bodily gestures that emanated from him were also having a detrimental effect on the performance of his whole team.

Jane's fear froze her natural ability to perform to her optimum level and it frustrated her. The intensity of her disempowering block appeared to be insurmountable to her.

I know that changing our state often collapses reactions like these. In view of this, I recommended that she used the stimulating algorithm before her presentations. I recommended this because I knew that stimulating those points was likely to facilitate her performance and this would inspire those present. She practised with this algorithm for minor situations to see how it felt for her; then she used it the next time she made a presentation.

Jane reported to me that, during this presentation, she was lively and energetic, and was able to look around at her colleagues as well as at her boss. She told me that she knew that her own more animated body language, facial expressions and upbeat self-belief changed the state of this entire group. She was absolutely thrilled by this because it gave her great personal enjoyment, and it enabled her to deliver other projects.

Jane continued to use this algorithm when she wanted self-confidence and the wonderful energetic buzz which enabled her to look forward to presenting to others.

A couple of months later she came to see me again and asked if there was a way in which she could develop more healthy independence. She loved to help family, friends and colleagues. However, she was becoming increasingly aware of her intense need to please others. This meant she was often unable to say no and ended up feeling anxious inside as well as fearful of upsetting others when she said she couldn't do something. I recommended that she used the sedating algorithm at times like these before she actually responded to other people's requests. She told me that doing the sedating routine gave her time for reflection and for her to make wiser decisions; the effect of the algorithm was very relaxing too.

Journal reflection:

Have you thought of times or places where using one, or both of these algorithms could benefit you too? If so, write a few notes or a list of possibilities in the front of your journal. Then later, after experimenting, jot down some of the most interesting results.

Examples of surrogate tapping

It would always seem respectful and ethical to ask permission of the friend, or the parents of a little one. And for recipients who may not be well enough to ask for healing, it can be sent prefaced by "If this healing is meant for you or if this is right for you, then let it be so." An attendee at one of Gary Craig's seminars asked Gary if he thought it was unethical to be sending surrogate tapping without asking for the client's permission. His reply to this was "When you feel anger, or negative thoughts and feelings towards someone, do you ask their permission to send that?" This made immense sense to me … and I still like to ask permission if it is at all possible to do so.

Tapping I transmitted to a client whose relationship was floundering

Sara rang because she was so distressed about the way her relationship was heading. We took time to reduce the intensity of her distress by tapping a little together.

At the end of her phone call with me, I said to Sara, "Would you like me to send you surrogate tapping healing later on today?" She said yes. I then knew she was happy for this to happen.

Throughout that day, I tapped on myself whilst thinking of Sara.

EB point: "Even though Sara is very upset, no wonder she feels sad, what if doing this could help her?"

SE point: "I open my heart now and send healing love and comfort to her."

UE point: "Maybe Sara will sense that somehow this sadness can and will pass as it has done at other times in her life."

UN point: "I imagine seeing her now, gently wrapping her arms around herself with loving kindness and compassion."

CHIN point: "What a remarkable difference her self-compassion will make to her state of mind and body!"

This was the initial surrogate healing that I sent. Then I continued to tap on myself on her behalf, and say whatever came to me.

That evening Sara sent a text to me that said, "Thank you, Mair, I know that you have been holding me in your heart today – I feel so much calmer now."

Surrogate tapping for animals

Surrogate tapping on a dog called Kim

Early on in 2000, a vet, Marie, came to one of our EFT training courses. She wanted to learn EFT for her animal owners and her animal clients as well as for those who helped and supported her in her clinic. The problem which this vet brought to our training was related to animals that were experiencing separation anxiety whilst they were recovering from surgery.

In addition to this, Marie had recently learnt that her own little dog, Kim, seemed to be troubled by separation anxiety as well. One of her neighbours had mentioned to her that Kim cried frequently and was very distressed when she left to go to work in the mornings. After hearing about this, Marie tried a number of strategies but none had any impact on Kim's reactions. After completing her EFT training and learning about the benefits of using surrogate tapping, she decided to do this the very next time she left Kim at home.

We recommended that soon after leaving her home, she find somewhere safe to park her car and tap right then. The benefit of doing this at that time was that whilst she tapped on herself in her car, her little dog would still be upset about her leaving. Doing the tapping when there is no disruption in the other's energy system is unlikely to help. However, tapping when Kim was likely to be unsettled would land a lot better.

Two weeks after her EFT training, she sent us a thank-you card for the successful results of her surrogate tapping when she left home the day after her EFT course. Her next-door neighbour had recently popped around to tell her that there had been no more crying or barking coming from her little dog next door since then.

Surrogate tapping for a pony

A horse trainer called Carol rang one day to ask about ways to help her little pony, Star, who had sustained a painful accident with barbed wire in the field where she lived. Her physical injuries healed well; however, since this little one's painful experience she had become very jumpy. Carol said a vet had told her about surrogate healing and she wanted to be able to help by learning how to do this herself. She also thought it would be good to know what to do in other circumstances in the stables she owned.

Whilst she was on the phone to me, I asked her for more details about Star's accident so that I could give her examples of how to use surrogate work in the future. I learnt about how the wire had caught and trapped her and she had fought her way out of the entanglement. Unfortunately, no one was around when this happened. So, she was left on her own for quite some time after the accident because nobody knew she was hurt. This was a major part of what had happened and now Carol was traumatised too. I decided to do some EFT on Carol's feelings straight away with her whilst tapping and talking. She admitted she felt guilty not knowing that Star had suffered alone for so long, and she blamed the extent of the injury on herself.

Carol said she was an 8 and described how the feelings of guilt were in her throat and made her feel like crying.

SUDs 8 set-up statement – We both tapped on the KC point together and said three times, "Even though I feel choked with unshed tears and guilt, I have been doing the best I could for Star since she was hurt."

SUDs 9 – The reminder phrases for Carol were "I blame myself, how could I let this happen to little Star?" "I want Star to trust me." "I need to let this blame go." "She's picking up on my guilt and sadness." "What if letting this go could help her – and me too?" "What a difference this could make!" Whilst Carol talked, we each tapped on our face, body and hands at the same time.

SUDs 6 – Carol then wanted to do surrogate tapping and send it to Star from herself. As she was doing this on her own, her reminder phrases were "I will help you, dear little Star, by doing this every day, in the best way to help you that I can." "This will calm you and let you trust me once again." "Your little body and every part of you can relax now."

SUDs 2 – After doing this on herself, Carol sounded calmer and was able to let go of many of her unshed tears which she said was a great release for her. After we said goodbye, I emailed her a copy of our EFT chart so that she could use it in the future.

One month after our phone conversation, I received a lovely letter from her with thanks and praise for the benefits of the surrogate tapping technique. She reported that Star was her old self again and she herself was also happy and free. Carol had continued to tap each day on herself and was able to let go of all of her guilt. She had also begun to include tapping to build up her self-confidence as she knew she had done the best she could, given the circumstances. She found that caring for herself in this way embedded more self-care inside herself too.

Just thinking about doing the tapping can benefit you too

Our brief introductory courses in EFT are often two hours long. Usually there is a demonstration on those who have pain or stiffness (when they have already received medical checks). Someone who had already attended one of these courses rang to book on one of our EFT weekend courses. When I asked how she was, she laughed and said that if her shoulder became stiff, she just said to herself "even though" (the initial words of the set-up statement) and her stiffness always went away.

Another friend told us that when he just imagined doing the tapping without doing anything, he was surprised that his anxiety subsided! Both of these examples illustrate the power of our suggestion, expectation and imagination. Why not explore this more yourself and see what you come up with?

Anna, a psychology student and a participant in one of our introductory courses, let us know that, as she was just imagining tapping on her face points whilst she was tossing and turning in bed one night, she found that she calmly drifted off to sleep. She continues to use this whenever she feels tense.

A simple way to use EFT

When we have a large or small group (and I often use it with just one client on their own too) who needs warming up, we ask them to separate from one another and firmly plant their feet and keep them planted for the duration of the whole exercise. This is because any movement of their feet or change in their posture will mean they will not be able to measure the difference they receive. Then we say to them, "Swing your arm around to the side to see how far you can reach. Now, register that point in the room, whilst continuing to keep your feet planted."

When they return to their original position, we get them to tap on their KC point a few times, saying: "Even though I can only reach this far, I'm OK." Then whilst their feet are still planted firmly, we then ask them to once again swing their arm to see where they can reach now. Frequently there is a gasp when they realise how much further they can reach now.

Borrowing Benefits

Gary Craig began to notice that the individuals in the audiences he spoke to in seminars were experiencing benefits even when he was working on one person on the stage. As a result of this, Gary began suggesting that each person in his audience think about one of their problems they would like to address, write down the SUDs intensity of their problem on a piece of paper and put it under their chair on the floor. As Gary tapped on the client on the stage, he asked the audience to tap along with this person's experience – not their own.

At the end of his demonstration, during which the client on the stage experienced significant benefits, Gary asked members of the audience to check the intensity level they had written down and to put their hands up if they noticed that they too had received benefits from tapping. There were very few people who did not put their hand up. He did this often in his seminars. This is an interesting exercise as the problem of the person on stage is vastly different from many of those in the audience. However, this doesn't seem to alter the benefits that are received.

In another of Gary's seminars, I decided to measure how much I could improve my eyesight when borrowing benefits, so I wrote "improved eyesight" and my SUDs was a four. I think this was uppermost in my mind as I had my optician's appointment already booked for when I returned to the UK. I then forgot my intention until I visited my optician for my eye-test. My optician said to me, "What have you been doing, Mary? How come you can see this now?" When I told him, he said, "Mary, you are a witch." Since then, I have continued tapping for my eyes, and my eyesight has continued to improve, even though I am not getting any younger! I used to wear contact lenses or glasses all of the time and now I only wear glasses when I drive – a dramatic difference.

There are many EFT Youtube videos and EFT recordings on practitioners' websites that you can use for yourself to borrow benefits.

Remember that, before starting, you need to be ready with your current SUDs level. You are measuring something you wish to receive help for. Even if the recording has nothing whatever to do with what you want help with that's ok, as you saw earlier in this chapter. Keep tapping and listening to the recording and afterwards, check your SUDs level again.

If you are helping a friend and using EFT, here is another way for you to share borrowing benefits, as you will be tapping on yourself whilst guiding them. Before they arrive, think of a benefit you too would like to receive. Write down the SUDs level of what it is at that point. When your friend arrives, ask them to think of a problem they want help with, ask them to measure their SUDs and then tap with them on their problem. Then ask them to check their SUDs level again before leaving. After they've gone is your time to check your own SUDs level. When we help a friend and we both do the tapping together we are both likely to feel better afterwards.

Your reflection point:

If you have already watched an EFT video and used borrowing benefits on yourself, why not write down your experiences and any benefits which you notice afterwards in your journal? Don't forget that you can enhance your self-confidence levels with borrowing benefits too! You can hold an important desired intention in a specific area you want to develop and then tap along with any EFT video!

Chapter Nine: A Brief Summary

In this chapter, you:
Learnt about six more energy therapies
Found out how to send Surrogate Healing to humans and animals
Learnt about Borrowing Benefits

CHAPTER TEN

Self-Confidence, Healthy Independence, And Interdependence

Take a moment to think of a time when you remembered life was simple and enjoyable and you felt self-assured. Notice within you, that you knew you could trust yourself and your decisions. Was this when you were young or later on in your life? Have you enjoyed experiences in an upbeat thriving environment, where you were inspired by some really positive results? Can you bring to mind some place or time when suddenly you felt confident in yourself for no particular reason? At that time, what events and challenges that were either new or familiar to you did you easily take in your stride?

Take a moment to look at your resourceful desires in the front of your journal. Do your peak times give you a taste of achievement and do they help recall times when your life was flowing well for you? Does it help you to imagine seeing and feeling how good it was for you? And, as you look at your entries in your journal, are there some examples you had forgotten all about? Situations of knowing you were capable and that you trusted your own ability? Our own recollections of confidence, strangely enough, can often be discounted or considered insignificant. I've seen this tendency in myself, my students and clients. Is this true for you, too? If so, when you notice you are doing this, gently acknowledge this self-confidence and trust that are always there.

When you do this, the way you felt at that time as well as other positive associations that you identify can fuse together into worthwhile and powerful connections to use. Then your own awakened awareness opens up a highway into personal states, places and times when you felt confidence and self-support. You may have pictures in your mind, or a gut feeling in your body. At other times you realise you are using an inner conversation experience of just knowing that you are capable of completing a project.

Unhealthy and healthy Independence

Unhealthy independence is something we may end up subconsciously choosing; this is usually due to an earlier time of being hurt or bullied and it is there, ready and waiting for our own protection. Our needing to be extremely self-sufficient is a decision we make after learning that it is not safe to trust or ask for help. We try so very hard to make things happen and then become exhausted because we wish to be perfectly self-sufficient. When we spend lots of time on our own, we think doing this means we will gain additional freedom. Other people watching us often think we look like we are super cool. At times like this, even if we are struggling, we would never think of asking anyone for help. Unfortunately, being independent in this way has a massive downside. It won't allow us to feel, to trust, or even allow intimacy and we may well have a genuine fear of making any commitments.

The opposite of the above is choosing consciously healthy independence, and here is where we seek out and enjoy support and give back to others too.

A client discovers self-confidence and healthy independence

Gill came to me saying how negative she felt. When I asked her about her sad and happy memories, she said there were no positive empowering ones that she could recall. It is not that unusual at times for any of us to be blinkered in seeing or feeling that our life is like this.

Gill and I worked with her hurts using EFT, and she seemed to relax and open up a little. We then explored a number of areas where she might have felt confident or independent, but to her they all felt like a brick wall.

Then I asked her if someone had brought her to my consulting rooms or if she had driven herself. She dismissed her driving skills as something that everybody does. I said to her, "Have you ever driven somewhere that felt interesting and enjoyable for you?" She admitted that she loved driving in Europe and frequently did this whilst on business. Her driving-in-Europe experiences were long before any SAT NAVS were available or possibly even thought of. To me, that illustrated a lot of confidence, as well as the ability to react independently and to do well. I said to Gill, "I love driving but I just cannot imagine how I would travel across Europe on business alone. However did you do it?"

We found that all of these years of her discounting her skills and many of her qualities had been part of her childhood conditioning. On so many occasions she had been criticised for being happy about her achievements, and these experiences had confused and saddened her. In many ways, parents and teachers do discourage children from bragging – and for good reason. However, Gill had not been bragging: she was just sharing her delight with what she had accomplished. And the severity of the reproaches she had experienced had hindered her from developing confidence and her self-belief.

As we worked together, Gill found that she was able to link into her resourcefulness again. For any of us to create healthy independence in a novel setting, we need the association of a time, a place or a feeling of where something worked well for us before. If we have been encouraged to explore and have a go at experimenting with fresh experiences, then we already have the skill and the backing to do this again. This gives us a known way to push back the boundaries of a new experience more easily. Knowing how we wish to feel or react in the new situation is like a template that will inform us again. When we reflect on our realistic associations, they take us in the right direction at other times. It is essential for us all to connect to an energetic state of being – of feeling, seeing or knowing that we have achieved a worthwhile outcome, however small it may have been.

Gill followed up on her powerful and enjoyable European journey memories just before sleep. As she explored and relived many happy carefree visits, she began to feel so much lighter. Although these feelings were still a little unfamiliar to her, it illustrated that the shift in her perception was still happening. Gill's wonderful associations that related to the places she had visited were now dramatically deepening her level of confidence. On her second visit, she reflected on how much more comfortable she was – even socially. She described ways in which she was willing to really nurture her growing confidence and healthy independence.

This new level of living opened her up to dismantle her fixed boundaries and to explore. Previous to our sessions, she never looked anyone she came in contact with in the eye. She now really looked at her colleagues and the lady at the supermarket. She found doing this helped her to make a connection to others, and she enjoyed that a lot. Expanding her life also helped her to enrol on a course and to discover more about the other members on the course. She knew this was happening to herself. She knew she was expanding because she felt more joy; it lifted her heart and cleared her mind so that life flowed like a mountain stream. Some months later, she sent me a card expressing how well she felt in all aspects of her life and work.

Locating a time in your own life when you too felt more confidence

As you have now read Gill's experience in locating a time when she was confident as well as happy driving in Europe, maybe you have found something similar in your own writing at the front of your journal. Perhaps a glimpse of a gem when you felt enjoyment or you learnt how to get results whilst being able to help others. It certainly does not need to be a dramatic event – often simple shifts in our perception can happen from someone who encourages us. Perhaps a dear adult helped you learn to ride a bike. Then, afterwards, were you surprised to find out they had stopped holding your saddle and you were still confidently cycling on your own?

Trusting yourself to do something to the best of your ability will take you through to enjoying more confidence, and to accessing your desired state again. Often these require mini-steps. I notice it helps me when I use positive words or sayings to myself such as: "I'm on my way, I'm getting there, I can do this, Easy-peasy," or even, "Where there's a will there's a way!"

When you can let these images, words, sounds, feelings and memories in, they are phenomenal ways to support and care for you. Showering yourself with kindness, patience and understanding opens up love towards who you are. Now, you may be saying, "That's easy for You to say, Mary!" because sometimes our very last reaction is to open up with kindness. However, when we can do this, it supports us beautifully and lifts us beyond our experience of being not good enough.

These kindnesses will be indelibly printed in your heart and will become frequent companions available to you. Other people's upbeat comments will also support you and are unique keys to opening doors that enhance your growth and self-belief. Gill became aware of this happening on the course that she joined. Her confidence and her desire to open up to other members meant she received their friendship. She felt valued for her genuine interest in others and the helpful suggestions she willingly gave. She felt so much appreciation and the group also benefited from her wisdom.

How my own confidence grew during my cancer treatment

I am more confident today than I was in early 2009. Throughout that year I took loving and kind responsibility for my life and my health when I discovered a lump in my breast. I usually checked my breasts in the shower fairly regularly. However, this time I woke early and whilst lying in bed I found this lump. It was as if I was meant to wake up and find this at that time. My first reaction was to do some EFT tapping on my fears that were gathering round. This supported and helped me to be clear about what to do– which was to see my local doctor that day.

My doctor immediately referred me to the local cancer clinic and she reassured me by saying "It's maybe nothing." At the time, I felt calm and almost like I was held in safe hands. It also seemed as if I was on a path that I was meant to be on. After my biopsy, the cancer was confirmed and I still knew I was going to be OK whatever was going to happen. It was as if my self-belief and trust in my mind and body's ability to take care of me was an absolute certainty.

I regularly practiced self-hypnosis and confidently enjoyed visualising my body taking care of what was happening to me and supporting me in the treatment I received. Even after surgery and radiotherapy I continued to feel safe and my confidence blossomed. Frequently deep gratitude enveloped me for the finding of the cancer, for having it diagnosed early and for all the love and compassionate care I received.

On reflection, my journey through cancer and beyond has given me more understanding for others who need care and compassion at these times too. When people ask me how I felt about this time, I honestly say I would not have chosen to have cancer; however, I wouldn't have missed the experience for the world.

What happened within your own life that created your insecurities?

After reading Gill's story we know that what happened to her in childhood contributed to her severe lack of confidence. From this she learnt to discount any skills she enjoyed due to her early conditioned responses.

Without exception, many of us remember times when we felt less confident. As a ten-year-old, I innocently asked my teacher if I would pass the Eleven-plus exam. His bleak answer to me was "You're thick: you won't achieve anything." What do you remember? And as a result of this, were there occasions you held back from doing something because of your insecurity? It's right at these times that we need to practice choosing instead to be gentle and kind and to ask ourselves exactly what we would really love to do if we could. Our imagining or guessing is a big and important plus, even when it can seem rather a stretch. These intentional thoughts percolate over time, so, in asking, it is often so very likely for us to receive.

Lacking confidence can often be due to the beliefs we have learnt and still hold, outside of our conscious awareness. In my case, I already knew I was not good enough to achieve anything, and because my teacher told me so, the belief solidified within me. I believed he was right, and this meant I left school without any qualification. So, for some time after that, seeking ways to gain experience felt scary. Fortunately, though, when we are patient and understanding with ourselves, we receive support, safety, and amazing openings. It can help a lot if we just think of how we would talk to an anxious child, as many times our fears have originated in early life.

After moving to another school at twelve, I was very surprised as well as reassured when the headmistress openly explained to us new pupils that she couldn't spell, so she always carried a dictionary. Her honest attitude opened the way for me to feel safer and my confidence grew enormously whilst at that school. I later realised that my self-acceptance increased as I encouraged myself when the going got tough.

Healthy Independence

Louise Hay: *Healthy independence saved my life – it gave me the courage to leave home at fifteen and to escape from abuse.*

My first experience of learning about healthy independence came to me when I saw that headmistress of mine confidently carrying around a dictionary. What does independence mean to you? How would you describe it if you were asked? Have you met friends who seem to have healthy independence? When talking about them, would you say they get on with their lives because they have self-respect? I believe that without this, Louise would not have had the strength to leave home when she was so young. When we respect ourselves, we take care of ourselves too. When you think about taking care of yourself, does it conjure up good feelings? My own, and not necessarily the dictionary definition of self-respect, is about being connected to your true self, your personal power, and your learnt resources.

Independence can give you freedom of choice as well as belief in your personal capabilities. Do you recall a time when you really needed support and there was no one around to turn to? Were you at that time of your life able to support yourself with healthy independence as Louise did? If so, that shows just how determined you are. If you believed in your ability and supported yourself in carrying out a task, this sense of knowing can be easily accessed now, and again in the future. When you need it, and you recall it with all your associated upbeat feelings, then it will be there for you to feel your support again.

Reflection point:

Notice and connect to exactly where you remember feeling that sense of knowing.

After taking time to capture this, it will highlight a far deeper connection to your experience of success.

Then tomorrow, or next year, when you need it, you will easily prime your recall.

It can be a physical feeling of knowing you are capable.

Whenever or however you experience an expression of your healthy independence deep inside, you have a knowing that you are and always have been dependable.

Your trusted expectations in yourself mean that it is very simple to transfer skills from an earlier experience to another time or place.

Whenever you reflect on your personal competences, your heart-centred process and your intentional practices provide a wonderful way of giving yourself positive feedback on your progress. Appreciating how well things are working out for you is a powerful way to strengthen these abilities. Gratitude impresses valuable experiences and creates knowing's in your brain as well as your body of just how far you have come. This then means it is possible to utilise the same strategies on new unexplored areas that you wish to pursue in your life now, as well as at some future time or place.

Saying yes to one of life's opportunities

The important part of developing new strategies or skills involves knowing in detail what we are wanting even if we are unsure how to make it happen.

I was afraid of speaking in public, and I wanted to develop confidence in presenting. That was one of the reasons I spent time watching and listening to an excellent presenter that I was shadowing at a deputy head teachers training course held in South Yorkshire in an adult training centre. I had been invited to watch and learn from this presenter as part of my professional development. She was an inspiration, as well as a well-respected senior psychologist.

On the day I was driving to her lecture for my fourth visit, a strange thought or feeling came over me. I sensed that she would not be there, and I wondered what I would do with this group if she didn't turn up.

As I continued on my journey, I imagined how I might handle the lecture myself. Different possibilities came to mind of what might work or be appropriate for this group. Then, on arrival, I sat at the back of the room, waiting to listen to her as I had done before.

When the head of department arrived, he came straight to me and said, "Can you take the group, Mary?" and I immediately said, "Yes!" even though fear struck me quite forcibly. When I asked him where he would be if I needed him, he answered "Here, at the back of the room." Knowing this only added to my anxiety. I felt that I wasn't at all like this experienced tutor; however, I knew that I would have to just be myself. As I introduced what we would do together, I sensed that this group were really accepting of me. Experiencing their warmth brought feelings of appreciation to me for their kindness and this helped me to relax. I knew without a doubt, then, that this was something I really wanted and was passionate about doing.

This experience led me to teaching psychology in many colleges, schools and universities and it was something I really loved doing. And at the time, this new venture helped me enormously because of my recent move to South Yorkshire. I had just introduced my former clients and my private therapy practice to another psychologist in the Midlands who was to take over from me. The new teaching contract that I was given after taking this group unexpectedly bridged the gap between my giving up my private practice and this new and beautiful opportunity.

My being open to new opportunities created a window of possibilities, and during my drive to the college, I had had time to air the chances of something opening up. Living with an open mind allows us to notice fresh choices that are always around us.

How about another dip into a reflection time now?

Practicing yes:

When was the first time you said yes to something and then the results delighted you?

Has saying yes without really thinking about things in too much detail been good for you too?

Have you ever found yourself refusing to do something and then at the last moment you decided to change your mind? What did you discover from your change of heart???

Before you go… jot down a word at the end of these questions which will help you to recall your own yes exercise. It can be something you thought about yourself, a comment by others or something a friend reminded you of.

INTERDEPENDENCE

Perhaps you have watched birds helping one another in flight. I learnt recently that when geese fly in formation, they can fly 70% farther and at a much faster speed than they ever could alone.

After living in the Midlands for twenty-five years, and Tam and I found ourselves transplanted in South Yorkshire, I knew that I needed to stretch my comfort zone. It was certainly fabulous fun to move into an old converted barn in a beautiful lively village and to put some roots down. However, we knew nobody, so I was starting from scratch again with beginning my therapy practice and this was a challenge. I really missed my busy practice, and my social life.

Tam and I soon began to make contacts in our friendly village. It was far easier than we thought it would be. We found ways of getting together with a number of other therapists who practiced in the village. To our surprise even the couple living next door were both reiki healers so they and others welcomed us with open arms. The joint support and encouragement towards one another meant that we all became stronger. Then even more like-minded others became involved. Each of these new connections added other dimensions and these soon fostered truly novel opportunities and fresh ideas.

Very soon we made plans and joined together to run evening taster events which included sharing and getting together in one another's homes. We welcomed anyone who was interested to come at no cost for an evening together with supper to follow. These became very popular – so much so that a local writer and historian frequently attended and included news of our events most weeks in the local newspapers. He also managed to compile a book related to many local worthies.

Interdependence is hugely important for the health and growth of any business or village community. It encourages creativity and opens up unique choices that on a one-to-one person basis may never occur.

If you are in a new situation and out of your comfort zone, take your time in gathering support; connect a little bit at a time with a group that interests you, or with a like-minded and supportive community. Are there interests you have not had time or confidence to pursue before? Libraries often offer possible interesting options.

Having the intention initially to practice friendliness can be a wonderful beginning to help you to open up. It may be a chat with someone waiting at the doctor's or in the post office queue, or a friendly smile for someone's lovely little puppy when out walking. Small steps are excellent ways to get past your reticence to start a conversation.

One book that helped me many years ago was Dale Carnegie's *How to Win Friends and Influence People*. It was about creating relationships with others, and about really listening to, as well as talking about, the other person's interests. When we can relax and just listen, it becomes easier and we can learn from this. When we connect and show genuine interest in others, trust develops. This offers us an excellent way to help, support and share as well as to learn and grow with one another.

Journal reflection points:

Now, take a moment to write down three enjoyable memories that you have treasured recently in the front or middle of your journal.

Whilst looking back over a few weeks – how did your opportunities begin to take shape? Where in your life did they benefit you?

In what ways did these open up fresh choices or possible additional experiences?

Were friends involved and if so, did it add another dimension to your joint venture?

Write about these in the front of your journal: they may well continue to support and inspire you to even deeper levels of living through your own personal journey of self-discovery.

Chapter Ten: A Brief Summary

In this chapter, you:
Saw the difference between unhealthy and healthy independence
Learnt how a client developed self-confidence
Read examples of the benefits of interdependence

CHAPTER ELEVEN

Heart-Centred Nourishment For You

Being Compassionate towards Yourself

Over the last few years I have become aware that I may not always be as understanding towards myself as I am to others. How thoughtful are you towards yourself? Do you give yourself love and consideration? Making time to understand how we are opens up a way to bring warmth and encouragement inside. One reason why we don't take care of ourselves may be due to early experiences of thinking we didn't measure up. Our parents, teachers and siblings may have thought it was appropriate to correct us. Perhaps we misinterpreted it? Perhaps the intention was to teach rather than criticise us?

As a result of my experiences, I believed that loving myself was selfish. Now, I know that it is of great value to care for our personal wellbeing. When we do, our love and our desire to care are intuitively felt and enjoyed by those lives that we touch. It also means that we can feel able to contribute to others by sharing, among other things, our learning with them.

When we can talk about our experiences of moving past our blocks, a bond is created – it's like we are on the same page and we speak the same language.

Perhaps you are already familiar with nurturing strategies to support your wellbeing. If, however, you are looking for additional benefits to your health and vitality, I recommend Dr David Hamilton's delightful book entitled *I Heart Me.* It is touching, interesting and easy to read. David's honesty is heart-warming and the scientific background he shares is simple and practical. It has taken me a lot further along the path of understanding, and caring for, myself.

I am guessing that forgetting to say thank you to a friend, a partner or a colleague would worry you. It may be natural for you to gently touch someone's hand as a sign of appreciation. In what ways do we miss opportunities to be understanding and thoughtful to ourselves?

Having compassion and appreciation genuinely spreads warmth and understanding to ourselves, and to those close to us. I think of it like this. When a cup is filled to overflowing, it runs over the top. When we practise self-love, it fills us up to overflowing with thoughtfulness and love. Then, whilst connecting to others, this love and understanding automatically reaches them too.

Does receiving kindness feel good to you?

When family and friends show love or give you gifts or complements, have you found that you are a little uncomfortable receiving them? In the past, I was often uncomfortable receiving and I think that said a lot about the limits of my self-care and love. My mother would often give and go without herself: she had an extraordinary giving nature. I think this worked well for her, but for me, as I adopted this behaviour unconsciously, it sometimes left me feeling unbalanced and empty.

If you experience discomfort in receiving, your giver may not even know that you are feeling this way. You may not even know why you feel this way. Could it be that you are unfamiliar with your own love for yourself? Do you think that the love and respect you could give to you would help you to feel relaxed and excited when you are on the receiving end?

An Exercise for You

Ask yourself, "How would I like to react when someone sends me a loving message that really surprises me or says something kind or complementary?" Think of being excited, touched, and happy as well as appreciative to receive. Let your mind wander around this for a while.

When you gave your friend a thoughtful, funny or loving gift and you watched him reacting with surprise and happiness, how did that feel for you? Were you both laughing and enjoying time together? Were you thrilled that you had managed to buy something that he really loved? Just notice next time, that what you give out comes back to you.

After trying this exercise, why not write a little in your journal so that you can be aware of your ongoing benefits?

Forgiveness

There is a lot of confusion around the word 'forgiveness' and around the situations where forgiving would be the ideal thing to do. For very valid reasons, we often resist even considering the choice to forgive as a possibility.

We may feel confused or angry and all of this is enormously distressing. We may be unable to see a viable way out of our stuck state. Each one of our emotions is a huge block to our letting go. Mostly what we do is repress our discomfort whilst trying hard to ignore what actually happened. At other times, we justify what we have chosen to do in our own head, thinking that what we did was the only right possible course of action.

I found myself resisting forgiving someone once and it caused much sadness and distress to that other person and to myself too. It was a very painful and immensely worthwhile lesson for us to learn. Forgiveness happens when we are able and willing to let go of judgement. However, the timing of your forgiving needs to feel exactly right for you. I knew I wanted to be at peace with what had happened but there was still fear. To help myself I imagined an opportunity opening up for me and then the right time happened for us both.

Recently I watched the film *Walk to Freedom*. Towards the end of this film, as the time came for Nelson Mandela's release from prison, he was asked a question. The essence of the question was "What are you going to do now that you have your freedom? Will you want revenge?" The love in Nelson's voice when he answered was truly astonishing. It was obvious from what he said that he had already forgiven those involved in what had happened to him, a very long time ago. He also said, "If I hadn't forgiven them, then I would still be in prison."

Self-Acceptance

After listening and writing down my thoughts and feelings in my journal and exploring the importance of self-acceptance, it became evident what this word actually meant to me. It's more about understanding the whole of who we are, and being open to this means "who we are" includes our perceived faults and insecurities, our vulnerability and our strengths. And from this it's possible to see that we are all so amazingly different and that comparing ourselves with others is not kind, helpful or nurturing at all – and it's impossible to do!

Appreciating our own self-acceptance state – even when we are struggling or as high as a kite – is the road to being increasingly accepting of others too. When I am loving and appreciative of you, you and I know this feeling inside instinctively. We feel the ease and joy of this even though it may not be expressed. We sense our connection and our mutual harmony. There is no need to actually voice this, although of course it is lovely when we do.

Reflections

Think about enjoying a deep connection with someone. As you do this, who comes to mind? As you look closer at them and at the situation, what are you saying and how do you feel about them? What makes them special to you? Is it the way they look at you or how they listen? Are they compassionate and kind? Are they easy to be with? Do they look on the lighter side of life?

And as you continue to think about this person – what sense elements are involved? Do you feel you can be yourself when you are with them? Are you happy knowing that you can trust them? Do you think this person has respect for you? Does your experience of knowing that you have a connection, or are in tune together mean you are relaxed together?

Imagine again your thoughts and answers from the above reflection exercise. Then, ask yourself if the person you were thinking about helped you towards increasing your own self-acceptance. Do you want more examples of feeling comfortable inside yourself and the chance to deepen your own self-acceptance?

When we choose to be patient and accepting of ourselves, our feelings of self-worth have the chance to develop. Our ensuing ease allows us to build bridges and enjoy positive reactions from our own experiences that we can then share with other people we meet. It makes a noticeable difference to the flow in our own lives.

Writing about emotions – a part of healing

Here is a simple (and heart-warming for me) example of how my self-acceptance made a big difference to my life. I had been writing a piece that was emotionally very close to my heart. This began as an exercise during a writing course, when the tutor asked the group to write their transformational story. Mine was an emotional story around two pages long; it ended with little me opening up from the realisation of exactly what she had felt at around five years old.

I gave my story to someone for feedback, and when they told me what they thought, I felt that they hadn't understood what I meant. I felt hurt. This must have been obvious, because they asked me if I was alright. In the past, I would have said, "Yes, I'm OK thanks!" But this time it was different – I didn't say anything and I knew I wished to be alone to think about how I felt. I decided to wander into our local village. As I walked, I went inside gently to explore my feelings. I'd been thinking about inner child work, and I thought I would talk to my small self. And right then, I found myself having a deeply loving conversation with "little me." This was a truly kind and understanding moment that opened me up to a meaningful and loving connection to my inner child. I gently said to little me, "Darling little one, he (the person who had given me the feedback) doesn't and cannot know how you feel, because it's not something that has happened to him." My inner child said, "He isn't even trying to understand or think of how I feel!" I said to her, "If you feel that, no wonder it hurts! You're right: it's not ok. I love you, and I am learning to understand why you feel you have not been heard. I promise you that I will be listening so much more carefully to you now."

Immediately after our conversation together, I felt euphoric, uplifted and totally free – an experience that I had never felt at that level before. I had often noticed hurt, frightened and sad feelings inside and had not ever actually made such a deep and truly meaningful connection of talking so lovingly to little me.

When I returned home after my walk, I no longer needed to reject my reader's feedback. Something very remarkable had happened inside of me. My perceptions were no longer clouded by the trauma of past experiences. Now, I was open to welcome life, to let go and to grow.

This all occurred because I wrote something. I wish for you to find that your own writing can add to your own healing too, in ways perhaps that you couldn't even have imagined.

A journal exercise for you

Now you know why I suggest that you consider writing events, feelings and jotting down times of confusion or sadness as a way of acknowledging and genuinely understanding yourself. As you listen to your needs and become your very own trusted friend, you too will notice surprising shifts.

The back of your journal is an excellent place to write to extend compassion, understanding and love to yourself and recall happy or sad memories. It also creates the opportunity for self-care and opens a door to far greater understanding of early events that perhaps affected your life. This can be comforting and may well open the door to changes in your perception.

The Butterfly Hug

When Tam and I were presenting EFT to the Amicrisis group in Mexico, we discovered that a number of the medics and caregivers shared an interesting type of hug. They gave this special hug to the children to take home with them and to use on themselves after leaving their helper. This lovely hug ensured that the children had something that they could easily do to bring comfort to themselves when they were alone or sad. The helpers named this self-help gift "the butterfly hug," because it looks a little like a butterfly when you watch it being used.

Imagine you are looking at yourself in a mirror. Then, place both arms crossed on top of the wrists and put your palms flat on the opposite sides of your collarbones. Then, imagine you are lifting alternate hands a little like butterfly wings and gently tapping them back down. Do this whilst still resting your wrists on your chest. This is calming for children who have experienced distress – and, it can be helpful for anyone! Use it yourself and then you, too, will know just how good it feels. Tam and I love using this: it brings comfort when we are tense or emotional and we often catch ourselves smiling too.

Stimulating both the Gamut point and the KC point

One day, I was tapping on myself whilst a client was following me doing EFT on herself. After a few minutes, she became very emotional, and so she stopped tapping. Instinctively, I asked, "Is it ok for me to gently hold one of your hands?" and she nodded. I then held one of her hands in mine and with the same hand that was holding hers, I gently stimulated the Gamut point with my thumb and the Karate Chop point with my index finger. (This way was easy for me – you may find another way.)

Almost immediately she calmed down, and looking at her hand, she said, "What are you doing, Mary? It's so comforting!" Then, a little later, she said "Thank you, that was amazing!"

This was a first for me, as in most circumstances, I rarely do EFT on my clients – I prefer them to know it is they who are helping themselves. However, as this particular client's emotions were coming to the surface, I really wanted to clear whatever was coming up. However, I felt that tapping on her face and body at this emotional time could be too invasive, so I tried this new approach.

Since this experience, I have used it many times, when appropriate, in sessions. My clients also use it on themselves. They have used it when they are emotionally triggered by something that is said, or when watching a programme on TV. They also use it in meetings, keeping their hands in their laps under the table. No one knows that they are gently touching these two points, as there is no tapping or talking involved. You can do this for yourself, too.

Hypnoesitherapy

Dr Angelo Escuder, a surgeon, developed hypnoesitherapy. He discovered that when his patients were anxious or in pain, keeping saliva in their mouths helped them to feel calmer as well as more comfortable. He found that it helped them to relax as well as feel free from pain throughout their surgery.

When we feel tense or anxious, our mouths often become dry, and a dry mouth can be an indicator of the stress response. So, when we intentionally collect a little saliva into our mouths, it averts this reaction. Imagine we have lined up a row of dominos: if you knock one down, the whole row collapses into a heap. The stress response functions a bit like this. When we intentionally collect saliva in our mouths, it is like taking one domino out of the line, and it stops the others from cascading down.

Many of my clients who experienced fear and anxiety in the past have said there has been a noticeable stress reduction when they keep saliva in their mouths. This technique can be applied to many situations once it is learnt. One client, who had frequently experienced panic attacks whilst travelling, phoned me to say, "When I keep some saliva in my mouth I feel calmer and I now enjoy travelling!"

Take a moment now to intentionally collect a little saliva in your mouth. When you feel that your mouth has become dry, do this again. Practice this even when you feel calm and comfortable – it will then become simple for you to use without thinking about it. In future, when you find yourself in an uncomfortable situation, gently collect a little saliva until your anxiety or pain has passed.

Quick Anxiety Stopper

This procedure has been helpful in reducing anxiety when clients crave food, alcohol, drugs, cigarettes or when there are desires for retail therapy, gambling, overindulgent eating or other out-of-balance responses. When we feel anxious for whatever reason, we may use any of the above substances or behaviour to reduce or push down our cravings.

When someone is craving another whiskey or cigarette, they can choose to go through the routine. Using gentle pressure on the three groups of EFT acupoints again and if needed, again, takes no time at all and they will feel calmer. These three points have the capacity to stop cravings without having to go through a longer EFT tapping routine. The simplicity of this means it's quick and easy. The calming effect then allows us to choose healthier options. That's why it is often called the "Quick Anxiety Stopper." It is a quick and simple way to bring balance to our energy system, and it helps us to make wiser choices before we have drunk too many whiskeys. It is also a valuable technique for when you feel anxious or upset emotionally. In the last six months, one client found out that using this technique helped him to avoid overindulging whilst gambling. It surprised him that the intensity to carry on in his usual obsessive ways was dramatically reduced. This meant he was able to enjoy this pastime without it impacting on his life or his finances.

The three points for the Quick Anxiety Stopper

1.) Under both eyes
2.) Both collarbone points
3.) Under both arm points.

Using the pad of your thumb and your index finger of the same hand allows you to gently touch under both eye points at the same time. Then, just below on the collarbone points, you do the same with the thumb and index finger pads. Quite often the collarbone point may seem a little tender and that is normal. The last two points are under both arms so hug yourself with gentle pressure, each hand under the opposite underarm point. This sends a message of comfort and warmth so that you experience a sense of care and love as well as being there for yourself.

When we touch and care for ourselves or another person there is a release of oxytocin in our body that uplifts us. This is sometimes called the cuddle hormone. It creates happy, loving experiences from touch and feelings of appreciation as well as other heart-centred connections that feel good inside. When we feel empathy or we stroke a puppy it activates oxytocin too. Its anti-inflammatory properties relieve pain, promote healing and enhance our trust. Oxytocin also has the potential to relieve stress, lower blood pressure and improve digestion, including help for IBS. So, when you give yourself a hug whilst using the Quick Anxiety Stopper, this gives you the added benefit of oxytocin.

All of these acupoints can be accessed easily without anyone really being aware that you are doing this. No tapping or talking involved; just take your time and use gentle pressure on all of the three points one after the other together with a gentle calming breath in between.

Journal Reflections

All the exercises we've seen in this chapter are designed to help you to support yourself with upbeat thoughts. If you recall times of achieving these thoughts, why not write them, creating your own list in the front of your journal so that they become more powerful links to your own resourceful state. Then, when you feel low, you have your list right there to help you. How about writing a promise to yourself in a brightly-coloured pen?

> **One client's list**
> I love myself just the way I am
> I care for me by choosing healthy food to eat
> I am gentle, kind and patient with myself
> I listen to my inner voice of wisdom
> I choose to acknowledge my skills
> When I forgive, I experience freedom

Chapter Eleven: A Brief Summary

In this chapter, you learnt about:
Nurturing strategies for others
How you can receive gifts and feel self-acceptance

How you can let go and forgive, when the timing is right

The Butterfly Hug and other simple points for emotional and physical pain

Stimulating two comfort (or release) points: the Gamut point and the KC point

Hypnoesitherapy

The Quick Anxiety Stopper

Chapter Twelve

Meditative Ways To Help Yourself

Be present, appreciate life and experience your blessings

I have included meditative ways in this last chapter, even though it's a relatively recent addition to my life. I had always thought these practices meant sitting for a period of time in silence – and this was very difficult for me to do. But after reading Thich Nhat Hanh's books, I saw that there are simple and easily inclusive ways to meditate, and these have all added to the ease and enjoyment I feel now. I want to share some of these discoveries with you.

Thich Nhat Hanh is a Buddhist monk and Nobel Peace Prize nominee – see Resources section at the back of the book for more information.

Walking meditation

When you choose to practise walking meditation, keep it simple and let it be joyful, uplifting and reassuring for yourself.

To begin this, you may wish to use one of your own suggestions – an affirmation, or a powerful resource that came into your thoughts that you wrote in the front of your journal. Choose something that has really touched you. Often a simple, affirming quote can be really valuable.

Experiment with linking your breath to your rhythm of walking. Walk slowly and easily and breathe in, taking 2 to 3 paces, and then breathe out with around the same number of steps. Let your routine settle within your stride whilst breathing in through your nose and breathing out through your mouth. Initially you could practise this whilst walking around a room.

When you have made this easy and pleasurable, do your walking meditation in places you love. There is added benefit to walking barefoot if this is something you enjoy. Barefoot walking any time of the day is called grounding or earthing. It allows your body the opportunity to absorb free electrons that have powerful antioxidant effects. These protect your body from inflammation and pain. Earthing also speeds up healing and reduces recovery time from injury. The fact that barefoot walking relieves muscle tension means it is also helpful for headaches and gives us many other documented health benefits.

(For more details visit this informative website: <u>www. mercola.com</u>)

When I was dealing with breast cancer, walking meditation was extremely helpful and nurturing for me. And it gave me the perfect framework for incorporating a very positive message given to me by one of my clients after she knew I was going through cancer treatment. This is what she said to me when she talked about my treatment: "It will be a walk in the park for you, Mary." Her words were said with such conviction, that I just knew that this was one of the most powerful and inspiring messages I had ever received. Up until then, intellectually I had known that words could heal, and now I know that to be absolutely true from personal experience. Repeating the words this client gave me inspired me each time I used them.

Here is how I incorporated her very uplifting message to my walking meditation. Whenever I walked to the shops, picked up my grandchildren from school or walked for a longer time in nature, I chanted her words to myself silently or out loud depending on where I was at the time. I knew without a shadow of doubt that the conviction she shared with me carried tremendous energy and positive expectancy to the very core of my being.

When I saw this client again in 2014 and I mentioned to her how powerful and helpful her words had been for me, she was as visibly touched in 2014 as I had been in 2009. When I saw the impact on her and we realised how her words had made a huge difference to my state of mind and body, we were both in awe and wonder. Walking meditation and chanting is something that I continue to do with great joy.

Sonic Meditation

During an interval at a conference in 2005, someone I had never seen before rushed up and introduced herself to me. It was almost time for us all to be seated and she wanted to say hello, before she went to sit down. During our conversation, this lovely woman told me a little about a beautiful spiritual practice she had been using. The meditation she shared is connected to the seven chakras and to the sounds that are linked with them. The benefit of this routine is that you can meditate on the sound of your voice that is connected to your chakras. You should extend the last sound and give it a vibrational quality.

You may enjoy adding Sonic Meditation to your personal practice. If you do, here is how you can use it. Find a comfortable seated position during this meditation. You can cross your legs or sit on a chair and rest your feet on the floor.

SONIC MEDITATION

Sonic Meditation

Crown Chakra...............	MIME
Third Eye Chakra...........	NEEM
Throat Chakra................	MEM
Heart Chakra..................	MAM
Solar Plexus Chakra........	HOHM

Sacral Chakra.................. HOOM
Root Chakra.................... HUM

When I first practised this meditation, I started at the Crown Chakra and hummed **mime** three times. I then moved to the Third Eye Chakra and hummed **neem** three times. I continued this way until I reached the Root Chakra. You may vary your practice by starting at the Root Chakra, or at any other point that feels right to you. Simply hum one sound and move to the next chakra.

Recently, I've begun to sing the sounds up and down like a tune rather than an even tone for each chakra. I do this one sound at a time and move onto another sound and chakra in no particular order.

I never saw that beautiful young woman again. We spoke for only a few moments, and she had only the time to quickly sketch an illustration. What you see above is what was created later when I returned home. I honestly thought I would easily be able to find more information about this method of meditation practice; however, that has not happened yet. I have consistently enjoyed practising this in many settings and at different times.

If you discover any references about this I would really value your feedback. The only other reference I know about is in Tam's (Llewellyn-Edwards) book called *A Meditation Manual for Energy Therapists* – which has its own logic, because I shared this with him.

For your feedback, your questions or insights, please contact me at MairLLLL@aol.com or www.TickhillClinic.com

Mindfulness: Anytime, Anyplace and Anywhere

Do not dwell in the past, do not dream of the future,
concentrate the mind on the present moment.
Buddha

I thought being mindful meant sitting in silence for a period of time whilst repeating a mantra. I now know it can happen at any moment —and inside a moment. I may be washing dishes, preparing breakfast or walking upstairs.

If you realise that you are packing lots of busyness into your day and you wish to relax, here are a few simple suggestions. As you prepare lunch, notice how your toes feel when you wiggle them inside your shoes. When clearing up without shoes on, how cool does the tiled floor feel against the soles of your feet? Can you hear birds singing outside, or a clock ticking? These frequently ignored sounds and feelings can bring enjoyment to your here-and-now, and moments of presence can continue as you go through your day.

When your intention is to pay attention, and to enjoy each experience differently, you will take yourself to another level of being. Even the coffee brewing or the browning aroma of toast can be part of this new experience.

Opening yourself to mindfulness in this way allows you to be calmer, as well as much clearer, as you complete tasks. You may even be surprised by your efficiency and how this benefits all that you achieve. You may notice a marked difference to times of being scattered or thinking, "What have I been doing?" or wondering to yourself, "Wherever has my day gone?"

At times when you have become aware of your mindlessness, think for a moment and realise what a gift it is to take a slow relaxing breath in and say silently "I am here" and then, when you breathe out, you can think or say "I am at home within." This is a slightly different take on one of Thich's many beautiful suggestions. Another is to walk mindfully, counting each step together with the suggestion of really paying attention to how it feels. as you step forward and then paying attention to how you lift your other foot to continue your walk. This way of being encourages you to go inside yourself.

Eating mindfully can add delightful taste to each mealtime. It offers you time for appreciation and calmer digestion as you relish each mouthful – however simple your meal. An additional bonus: when you are present, you probably will never bite your tongue!

Our New York and Sedona visit soon after 9/11

Shortly after the events of 9/11, Tam and I went to America. This trip had been planned some months before. Very few people were travelling by air, and I did feel some apprehension about going. However, I knew that our visit was absolutely meant to be – whatever else was happening.

We had been invited to teach a small group in Sedona, NM. The therapist who invited us wanted us to live and teach with this group in her home. After this training, we had arranged to meet Gary Craig in San Francisco.

On the day that we left the UK and flew into New York, I felt deep sadness, fear and distress from the people surrounding us. My heart went out to them – they were numb from the trauma.

As we travelled on a bus, these feelings were all-pervading, and I experienced a strong desire to send love to these people. In that moment, I felt and saw how I could give love at such a complex time. The image I saw was of placing the heels of my hands together whilst tucking the ends of all of my fingers inside and as I did this, I noticed that both of my thumbs were touching one another on their outside edges. This brought me calm, and I felt love and comfort circulating to all those people around us.

I found tranquillity and relaxation in this position for most of the rest of our journey that day. We arrived in Sedona, and throughout the next two days we worked with this lovely group.

I had had no intention of sharing the experience I felt on our arrival in New York. However, when one person in the group expressed her distress, I realised that sharing the positioning of my hands that I had discovered was the right thing to do. They loved it and said how easy it was to use for themselves and for others wherever they were and whatever they were doing.

Pineapple Mudra

Tam and I left Sedona, and went to San Francisco to meet Gary. When he asked how we had felt on arrival in New York, I decided to show him what I now call "The Pineapple Mudra." He was interested and wondered if this was stimulating both hand and finger acupoints as well as both of the thumb points.

Since our visit to America, I have continued to use and share this easy way towards being at home and centred inside. One of the benefits of having this way of resting with the finger and thumb points touching is that it's so gentle to use. It offers a delightful opportunity to be more at peace in the moment.

The Gift of Breathing

*"Our breath is the bridge from our body to our mind."– **Thich Nhat Hanh***

From taking our first breath at birth until now, our mind/body breathes with unconscious competence. In most cases, nobody has deliberately taught us how to breathe. I have explored breath-work and yoga, and breathing with mindfulness and meditative techniques. I have found that the way I am breathing makes a massive difference to my enjoyment of life; I've also seen that I am more present in the here and now. It makes perfect sense to me now why people say that they "go home to themselves."

How about you? What have you noticed about the way that you breathe? Are you naturally relaxed with your breathing rhythm? Sometimes if you are tense do you find, like me, that you are breathing in the upper part of your body? This was something that I learnt to do when I felt stressed. If you want to make some changes in the way you breathe, you may find that just noticing your breath helps you to become aware of the free rhythmic gift that breathing slowly and mindfully will give to you. Here are a few gentle ways to settle yourself. They are supportive and no one will notice. They give you calm feelings when you want to be more relaxed.

Taking a calming breath in is a good place to start. Whenever you wish to, intentionally take a deeper breath in through your nose, and at the same time (if this idea resonates with you), think of a delightful and delicate aroma that you love. Notice how your in-breath settles you down a little. Then, as you breathe out through your mouth, slowly imagine blowing on a dandelion clock and then see all the seeds floating down. When you breathe freely, when you breathe slowly, it may help you to experience a settled sense of wellbeing inside. Think of it soothing you when you are experiencing tension, too.

As you practise and commit this and the other meditative processes to memory, they make way for you to be more aware, and to notice, as well as experience, appreciation in the here and now. These heart-affirming experiences can help with potentially challenging times and will open a way that is supportive. I recommend you practise them at home at first.

As they become familiar, they will nurture self-confidence in your daily life. Just being at "home inside" wherever you are, and whatever you are doing, builds healthy independence, resilience and compassion towards yourself and others.

An additional breath-calming routine

Your breath, when you are relaxed, is easy and unconsciously competent. However, when an unpleasant association triggers you, the ease of your breathing is often disrupted. You may also notice that it can affect your ability to talk naturally as well as to be yourself. Here is something you can do which will become second nature to you in the outside world after using it at home.

Sit, stand, or lie comfortably. Then, gently and intentionally let go and slowly breathe out any air from your lungs. You may be surprised that there is actually any in there. Then, freely take a pleasantly relaxing breath in and rest a little (holding that in-breath for a moment), then take a few normal slow breaths in and out at this point before once again letting go slowly with your breath out. If it is calming for you, you can gently empty all the breath out when you wish to. This is a process that may only need to be done once or twice before you return to your natural relaxed rhythm.

Many clients are surprised by how easy it feels to breathe in after letting their breath out in this way. In this exercise, you choose to intentionally breathe out gently whatever is currently in your lungs before resuming a gentle in-breath.

No one will know that you are doing this breath-calming routine with intentionality except you. However, your mind and body will pick up this message of your intention and this will transmit a reassuring state to every part of you.

Sleep rejuvenates you and benefits the health of your mind and body

For years I believed that if I slept too long, life would grind to a halt. Sleeping felt like a waste of time – I was inspired by so many opportunities. During my psychology training, I felt more alive than I ever had. Waking early before my four daughters woke up was a bonus that I enjoyed. My time for quiet study was a gift for me.

After completing my psychology course and building my private therapy practice, I was less driven. However, this made little or no difference to my sleep time. I had convinced myself that I required less sleep than most other people.

Now, with hindsight, I believe my lack of sleep contributed to my higher stress levels and was possibly a factor in my developing breast cancer. Even after that wake-up call, I still wasn't treating myself with the love and care essential to my good health.

This all changed for me when, completely out of the blue, I heard about an online course called "Thrive" (developed by Arianna Huffington). This word struck home forcefully. I knew deep inside that I was not thriving, despite helping clients to improve their quality of life. This course was my real wake-up call. Within a short time, it made a phenomenal difference to my life. The mind/body science wisdom underpinning the course convinced me without a shadow of doubt how essential sleep was for my health.

Before the course, I bought Arianna's book called *Thrive* and devoured it. I shared my enthusiasm with family, friends, clients, and my mentoring groups too. Everyone who read it found that it was packed with smart and simple suggestions. Many were practical, such as ensuring our alarm clock lights were off. I wanted to share some of the content of this book with you, and in this chapter, I'm just concentrating on sleep.

Here is a brief excerpt from Arianna's introduction:

"On the morning of April 6, 2007, I was lying on the floor of my home office in a pool of blood. On my way down, my head had hit the corner of my desk, cutting my eye and breaking my cheekbone. I had collapsed from exhaustion and lack of sleep."

Arianna's mother's words to her daughter

"I don't care how well your business is doing," she told her. "You're not taking care of you. Your business might have a great bottom line, but you are your most important capital. There are only so many withdrawals you can make from your health bank account, but you keep on withdrawing. You could go bankrupt if you don't make some deposits soon."

Here are some suggestions from Arianna's book for you to consider which could benefit your sleep:

Prepare your bedroom to enhance your peace with mind:
Remove all electronic equipment from your room.
If you need an alarm, if possible switch out or dim the light.
Avoid phone contact after 9.30 pm unless it's important.
Avoid reading emails and watching TV after 9.30 pm.
Keep your bedroom cool and if possible open a window.
Draw your curtains to darken your bedroom.

One of the following can be your before-bedtime routine way to wind down:

Take time to relax using easy breathing.
Listen to gentle, natural sounds such as those on a CD.
Take a calming, warm bath.
Practice a little yoga or gentle stretching.
When you are ready to go to bed, slip between the sheets.

Here are suggestions to help you relax:

Spend a little time practising self-hypnosis (i.e. imagining and remembering pleasant happy, calm times).

Do TAB from Chapter 9. Do this on your face points: touch your eyebrow, take a breath then slowly move onto the side of your eye and so on.

I began, just as Arianne suggested, to practise before-bedtime routines. And I have continued to do these. I included from the beginning no computer checks or late TV programmes. This gives me time for my yoga or, much more frequently, my self-hypnosis practice. Choosing to be more present and at one with my breathing naturally allows me to drift off into peaceful sleep. Now, I consistently go to bed earlier and wake after eight or more hours of sleep. This has given me more energy and has increased clarity in my thoughts. This routine is now a golden thread running throughout my life.

Chapter Twelve: A Brief Summary

In this chapter, you learnt about:
Meditative techniques
Being present and finding peace
A simple walking meditation
Sonic Meditation
Mindfulness, anytime, anyplace, anywhere
The Pineapple Mudra
The gift of breathing and the breath-calming routine
Arianna Huffington's suggestions for a good night's sleep

Conclusion

We have now reached the end of this book and our time together. We can think of us both as being enriched by times of reading as well as times of writing for ourselves in our journal. Your experiences and mine may well be different from now on.

Some Final Reflections

Decide on the best way forward for your continuing practice of writing and reflecting as well as listening to your desires, needs and choices. Even if you missed attending to this in some chapters, look back at your journal to see how much more you are able to add to what you are wanting to commit to. This is especially important for any practices that will benefit your health, harmony and more purposeful living.

Whilst I was writing this book for you, I noticed I was far more focused when I was committed to my own personal writing each day. I believe your writing for yourself in your journal will continue to be a constant companion to support you on your day-to-day journey.

I am very interested in hearing about your experiences and the intentions that developed as you read this book. I am also interested in hearing about how far you have travelled since you finished.

Because you have read this book, there is a connection that we have made, you and I. If you feel that you would like to, please contact me. If you live at some distance away or have difficulty phoning our UK phone number (01302 743113), you are welcome to email me at MairLLLL@aol.com or click the link to our clinic website: www.TickhillClinic.com.

On the website you will notice that I create personal CDs for my clients and students. If that interests you, please contact me.

Your commitment to your happy learning habits brings gratitude and experiences of love towards yourself. Your growing self-confidence takes good care of your joy in life. And very soon, you realise that you are becoming your very own best friend.

Appendix One

This chapter was written by me for part of a book called "EFT & BEYOND" that was edited by Pamela Brunner & John Bullough

Creating a Bridge to our History

Mair Llewellyn, EFT Master, EFTCert-Honors

Part 1: A bridge to our history

In 1980, when I first started working as a hypnotherapist with physical issues such as hay fever, migraine, asthma and IBS, I noticed that if I took my clients back in time while in a trance state, we were able in many cases to connect to memories of a time prior to the onset of their current illness or symptoms {see *Using Personal Resource States}*. It appears to be consistently true that our memories of healthier times remain intact, even after an accident, trauma or the onset of illness.

Later, I realised that I could use the same procedure with smokers to help them to quit smoking. Instead of creating a void by taking away cigarettes, we accessed early memories of the way they were before they began to smoke. This routine enabled clients to enjoy experiences of belonging and completeness without smoking, and the majority reported little or no cravings.

During the last nine years of using EFT, I have noticed that these same memory archive mechanisms can be accessed through the tapping procedure.

What about loss of mobility due to an accident?

For example, a client attended for help with loss of function after an accident. Following tapping on connecting to healthy memories from before the event, we discovered that it was possible for her to access more mobility via EFT than she had so far experienced through other therapeutic approaches.

It would appear that connecting to the memory and beliefs prior to the accident helped her to bypass tail-enders and link to an increased positive expectancy.

What about eyesight?

A number of clients have been able to improve their eyesight with tapping suggestions to access memories of clear eyesight from before the onset of their eyesight deterioration1. In some cases these recollections have been going back eyesight deterioration1. In some cases these recollections have been going back to the memories of five and six-year-olds, before glasses or contacts needed to be worn, enabling crystal clear visual memories to be tapped into.

What about strokes or spinal injuries?

By contrast, there appears to be little added benefit in accessing earlier memories with clients who have had a stroke. Perhaps in these circumstances, the memory in the brain has been damaged by the haemorrhage. However, this is not the case with spinal injuries which do appear to benefit from re- connecting to the memory before the injury. And in all examples it is helpful to do traditional EFT on the trauma, frustration, loss and fear.

What about other physical conditions and infertility?

Stress symptoms such as hay fever, migraine, IBS and asthma appear to improve faster by this method than for example by working on specific upsetting events and tapping to neutralise them individually.

A further very interesting part of my work is to provide support in working with infertility. This is particularly the case in circumstances where a client has undergone a termination, or following a miscarriage. Bridging a client's historical beliefs about their ability and worthiness in becoming pregnant is very beneficial. This is consistently the case when, for whatever reason the client has guilt connected with conception. On these occasions, for instance, if they feel (however illogically) that their original birth control method was detrimental to their conceiving, re-activating earlier memories of positive expectancy of the natural order of things can be an enormous help.

These observations reflect my experience in my own practice; I have not yet had the opportunity to conduct any controlled trials to test the results against other approaches. However, I feel that this method provides a very powerful way of (quite literally) tapping into the excellent resources we have stored in the archives of our minds.

This raises an intriguing possibility regarding a mechanism on how EFT works and why we tap on the negative. Maybe tapping removes the negative layer, thus exposing the original positive area below...?

Part 2: How to build a bridge to our history with EFT

THE IMPORTANCE OE PREFRAMING:

When we introduce our clients to EFT, we create a bridge from their existing knowledge of therapy or personal empowerment to EFT. When I introduce the benefits of accessing earlier memories of a behaviour or skill, I create a bridge specific POSITIVE events. These would be experiences, memories, images, sounds and feelings which they are wanting to reactivate. Asking clients to create a movie of that experience or memory and think of a suitable title strengthens their pleasant associations. Then, when a client taps while narrating their movie of physical or psychological well-being, its an even more powerful reconnection. Asking how long and how many euphoric crescendos were experienced is even better!

Throughout this whole time of choosing a movie title and tapping when talking and remembering the positive experience, it is very possible that any 'yes-buts' and tail-enders will have been successfully neutralised. Frequently I notice this happens even before we get to the stage of weaving in the positive suggestions with a more structured setup or reminder phrase. Perhaps when we move on to implementing this we are doing even more than we really need to, and the reconnection is already happening. Despite this, I am all for being thorough and I have always liked the idea of using 'belt and braces' (as we say in England). Or as Gary frequently puts it: *"Undersell and over deliver'.*

USE OF TRANCE:

Asking a client to think of a movie title for a positive past experience tunes them out from the here and now (their pain or trauma) and links them to the feelings, images, smells and sounds of that wonderful experience. When we daydream, or drive from A to B on a familiar route we tune out, yet we drive safely whilst we are thinking of something else. In a daydream, trance state, it is easier to gather information. Throughout any one day we drift in and out of this state frequently —at school we were told to pay attention by our teacher when we were daydreaming in a lesson. Within our minds, it is possible for us to experience our 'past', 'present', and 'future'. Daydreaming with intention can connect us to our previous healthy state, and tapping while using appropriate language facilitates this reconnection.

Can you give me a worked example?

In the example below, I have included language to help my client connect to the free feelings he remembers before he started smoking. This focused, specific tapping usually happens after feelings of being totally free have been accessed, as described in an earlier paragraph. My client decided on a movie title for that time. The movie was called 'Complete Freedom'. In all circumstances it is important to use your clients own movie title. Each therapy session is an energetic dynamic exchange. The setup and reminder phrase which come to mind in that moment reflect a clients wants and worries. In this way, it is tailor- made for the client.

When (and only when) the setup and reminder phrases resonate for the client, the conscious and unconscious mind connects to and recovers a healthier programme:

* *Even though I've been smoking for forty years, and I think I cannot stop, I deeply and completely love and accept myself anyway.*
* *Even though I started smoking to be part of the gang, I respect my teenage needs at that time—I was doing the best that I could.*
* *Even though I've been smoking since I was fourteen and I'm not listening to that teenage logic now because—I'm making healthy choices of 'Complete Freedom'.*

eyebrow: *As a teenager I wanted to belong to a group*
side of eye: *It's different now*
under eye: *Now, I want healthy choices*
under nose: *I cannot give up*
chin: I *can*
collarbone: *I really want to somehow*
under arm: *What if I could do this really easily now*
top of head: *What a difference that would make*

* *Even though I don't see how giving up cigarettes can happen - I've been a heavy smoker for 40 years now and I just cannot stop, I deeply and completely accept and forgive myself anyway.*
* *Even though cigarettes bring no genuine benefit to me—old habits are hard to change that's why I don't ever learn any new ones*
* *I choose to recover my 'Complete Freedom' now.*
* *Even though cigarettes have controlled me for 40 years—I choose to make today a really positive milestone and embrace my freedom again.*

163

EYEBROW: *I cannot remember being free of cigarettes*

SIDE OF EYE: : *I do remember—my movie title choice is 'Complete Freedom' and that's how being completely free of cigarettes feels*

UNDER EYE: *What if I connected to this 'Complete Freedom' programme again?*

UNDER NOSE: *It's my birthright*

CHIN: *What a difference that would make*

COLLARBONE: *Connecting to my health and vitality*

UNDER ARM: *Asking receiving and easily making the connections*

TOP OF HEAD *'Complete Freedom' is the way my lungs are intended to be*

* *Even though I don't know how I can do this, I do have this inner wisdom which I deeply and completely respect*
* *Even though in the past I thought cigarettes were my friend, I choose to create a more constructive feedback loop to optimum health and 'Complete Freedom'.*
* *Even though it's hard for me to consciously remember being completely free, my unconscious mind does remember, is my faithful servant and connects to the way I was meant to be right here and now.*

EYEBROW: *Recapturing my birthright*

SIDE OF EYE: *I really want my health instead of cigarettes*

UNDER EYE: *Whatever will I do with my hands?*

UNDER NOSE: *My hands remember being free*

CHIN: *I ask to be completely free*

COLLARBONE: *The way I was intended to be*

UNDER ARM: *Recovering my birthright*

TOP OF HEAD: *I'll be amazed and grateful at how good that feels and that good feeling gets better every day and in every way!*

Part 3: Further bridges to our history expanded

Let's now look at how this approach may be used with pain and physical problems. Any setup or reminder phrases which are used need to resonate with the clients own experience as well as relate to his desired objectives. I often say to my client: *"I want to know what you are wanting, not my perception of what you are wanting"*.

I believe that part of the art of delivery in working with EFT is being totally PRESENT with where your client is, right now—this includes what they are wanting from being with you in therapy. I have found that the technique of using NLP Time Line Therapy facilitates the process of accessing past wellbeing, whilst EFT provides an effective bridge to any shortfall here. In addition to this, accessing positive anchors or triggers strengthens the focus towards what clients are wanting. The combination of these client-centred approaches, together with aiming the setup to reactivate memories of wellbeing, provides a winning combination. To facilitate this healing we need to get ourselves out of the way. This applies to working on ourselves as well as working with clients. The following paragraphs briefly describe these concepts.

Why use time line therapy?

We exist in the past, present and future. On a moment to moment basis we are affected by memories, positive or negative. These memories can be from the past, or what we are experiencing in the here and now, as well as any possible future consequences of our current actions. That is why the healing work of EFT can create an awesome reframe when working on our history. This not only manifests change in the here and now but also brings benefits in the future.

The combination of using the NLP timeline technique together with EFT can be a profoundly effective bridge from past wellbeing to present and future emotional and physical contentment.

Why use NLP anchors?

Positive NLP anchors (associations or triggers)[2] provide a way to connect to a previously resourceful state so that that state may be cued at some possible time in the present or future. Cueing creates a link to past wellness, and is intended to reclaim and re-presence an earlier positive state of being. Re-connecting to the earlier state, to how we remember being, is our emotional, physical and spiritual birthright. When we re-ignite positive remembered anchors during the process of the EFT setup and reminder phrase, it often neutralises the yes-buts' and 'tail- enders' too.

Why get myself out of the way?

I have frequently found that when I have cleared my own 'tail-enders' to the limitless possibilities of true freedom, things happen. Getting myself and my preconceived ideas out of the way allows divine healing energy to flow freely. I encourage you to tap on yourselves for your own 'tail-enders' before doing this type of work with your clients.

Can you give me an example of these principles in action?

In this example a client we will call Pam described how EFT was helping her with her discomfort. The aim of working with this was to enhance the help that she was already receiving from EFT and to magnify it.

As Pam describes it: *"For myself I am dealing with arthritis, which somehow fortunately is at a low level I'm sure I have EFT to thank for that. It certainly helped to nip the last attack in the bud quickly."*

* *Even though I find that EFT can nip an attack in the bud, what if I could amplify the benefits even more somehow. I respect myself profoundly, I am doing the best that I can.*
* *Even though EFT helped to nip the last attack in the bud, what if I could go back before it ever began somehow, what a difference that would make—I honour my body forgiving me these messages and I'm open to the possibility of building a phenomenal bridge to my healthy past somehow.*
* *Even though I don't know how, I do know that my unconscious mind remembers comfortable joints and ease of movement because they are all in the archives of my mind—I ask, receive and allow that comfortable experience in again right*

now, and I'm willing to listen with even more respect to my body's messages.

Pam goes on: *"I do have to deal with an ache in my hips that comes while sleeping and actually wakes me regularly (that's about the worst discomfort with it). The remedy is to roll over onto my back and allow my hips to release, then I can fall back asleep again. I would love to be able to access my pre-arthritis body!"*

The following setups were used to link with this mechanism of Rolling over and her desire to access her pre-arthritis' body, while at the same time expanding on her experience of a physical release:

*   *Even though I would love to be able to access my pre-arthritis body and I'm excited about the possibility but I don't know how—what if that experience is there right therefor me to receive—how amazing that would be!*
*   *Even though I have learnt physical remedies which serve me well—of rolling over onto my back and allowing my hips to release—what if my mind could release whatever it needs to let go, naturally enabling me to receive added benefits? I know that in asking I receive. I respectfully ask now—just as I roll over and ask physically—thankfully and with positive expectancy allowing these added benefits to unfold.*
*   *. . . I accept myself completely, and naturally allow the abundance of added benefits to unfold, and I'm open to the possibility of being even more in tune with my mind body and spirit.*

I recommended that Pam ask for a laypersons description on her next official assessment with her conventional medical consultant. Understanding what happens within her body when it flares up, as well as when it settles down can be helpful. Gaining another person's perspective of a physical problem, as well as insight into how her joints would work if they were working well can be key to using EFT on the problem and connecting to relief.

When applying these approaches to your own life or the lives of your clients, the following points are valuable:

* When working with pain, medical check-ups are essential to rule out any issues which need to be addressed medically.
* Then, when you are ready to work with EFT, tune into how the discomfort feels for you physically and emotionally.
* Ask what was happening around the time the problem was manifesting. Ask what or who the feeling or discomfort reminds you or your client of. When the discomfort and emotional drivers have been adequately addressed, think of possible choices. Plan and use time line work to connect to freedom of movement and comfort.
* Create positive anchors of these remembered experiences. Throughout all of this work use EFT creatively and persistently.
* Aim setup statements and reminder phrases at current experiences of comfort, and build on them.
* Acknowledge each incremental step of improvement however small with thanks. When we do this it is like putting in a blueprint or signpost into the brain, directing the mind and body with the help of EFT towards more of the same.
* Use persistence to transform 'tail-enders' into understandable rational disbelief. You cannot lose anything by doing this and you stand to gain far more than you would even dare to ask for or imagine.

Part 4: Connecting to our birthright of fertility

We will now see examples from portions of sessions with two clients wanting help with improving their chances of fertility. These specifically highlight our endeavour to access their more positive mind-body connection. It is important to note that these two examples followed working in-depth on core issues. After your client reports emotional freedom on related issues, this is the most helpful time to make a reconnection to wellness.

Confirmation of freedom from trauma or negative issues can be assessed for you and your client in a number of ways:

* reaching a zero on the SUDs scale
* using a muscle test
* or even by testing SUDs in the real world.

Many therapists round off their sessions by using Pat Carrington's Choices. Following choices is an ideal time for your client to aim EFT at their future— and or to reconnect to their birthright of balance and harmony. When these approaches are used at this time, it frequently enhances the energy flow to associations of wellbeing.

How can I apply this process to infertility?

Fertility treatment is complex and often involves working with a group of health *care* professionals to discover what mav be going on. Conventional specialists often refer clients to me for help with possible emotional components of infertility.

Create positive anchors of these remembered experiences. Throughout all of this work use EFT creatively and persistently. Aim setup statements and reminder phrases at current experiences of comfort, and build on them. Acknowledge each incremental step of improvement however small with thanks. When we do this it is like putting in a blueprint or signpost into the brain, directing the mind and body with the help of EFT towards more of the same.

Use persistence to transform 'tail-enders' into understandable rational disbelief. You cannot lose anything by doing this and you stand to gain far more than you would even dare to ask for or imagine.

Case Study 1: Ann

Ann (not her real name) was one such client. She and her husband had been receiving many forms of fertility treatment without noticeable results. They were both feeling very stressed because it was not only costly financially but also emotionally. It was beginning to jeopardise their relationship. 'I asked Ann the following question: "If you were to guess at a reason why this is happening—however illogical it might seem—what would you say?" (This is a question I often use) Ann replied, as many do, almost immediately. The answer appeared to come to her unexpectedly and spontaneously from her unconscious. She said, "I don't believe that I will ever conceive because I have many feelings of shame surrounding becoming pregnant". Logically she knew that wasn't necessarily true. However, because her unconscious mind was running the show, not conceiving was what felt true for her at this point in time. Our initial sessions of therapy focused on using EFT to work on core issues surrounding this shame.

Ann believed that these core issues were the major block to her ability conceive. After freeing her of these limiting beliefs, we could have felt at this point that it was a done deal. However, I always remember Gary's motto: "undersell and over deliver". The following sessions of EFT with Ann included aiming EFT at the future as well as reconnecting to her inner wisdom prior to her trauma. Here are some of the setup statements which we used:

* Even though I know it was natural for me to conceive before my trauma, I deeply and completely welcome a reconnection now to my birthright during our loving oneness together.
* I deeply and completely honour my body's patience in allowing my mind to become ready to accept and nurture, so safely and completely, our baby within.
* Even though I don't know consciously how, I do trust the inner wisdom of my mind and body to naturally do what it needs to do to welcome and cherish our loved baby.

In addition to using setup statements and reminder phrases, I frequently encourage my clients to visualise their dreams, to include wonderful feelings and senses, and to tap whilst doing this.

Doing EFT whilst in a positive daydreaming state picks up any unspoken fears, and at the same time enhances the joyful positive expectancy of receiving.

Case Study 2: Di and Jim

In another case, Di and Jim (not their real names) were a couple who had been recommended to come to me by a fertility clinic some four hours' journey away. They arranged to stop over in our clinic and have intensive therapy over a three day period. During our introductions, Di told us that she had a somewhat reduced chance of conceiving due to the fact that she had had one of her ovaries removed in her early 20s.

The fertility clinic had assured Di, during assessment three years ago, that despite this they were very optimistic that she would conceive naturally. After three years of trying for a baby without result, they now felt concerned that their time clock was ticking and had returned to the fertility clinic for reassurance and guidance. Further tests were run and these provided reassurance that all was well, physically.

Even though Jim and Di came together, Di asked if I would talk to her on her own first of all. Jim talked and did EFT with Tam whilst Di and I spent some time alone. During our conversation she confessed that she had become drunk one night at a club and the following day as a precaution she had taken the morning after' pill. Five years later she was diagnosed with ovarian cancer. Di said that from that day until this one, she had always blamed herself for getting the cancer because of her recklessness.

While Di told her story, we tapped continuously on her distressing emotions. Afterwards, she explained that she had needed to discuss this with me on my own because Jim had always said: *"You were only young Di doing what teenagers do—give yourself a break"*. It wasn't that Jim belittled what had happened but intuitively Di knew that this guilt appeared to be a stumbling block to her conceiving. She said: *"I don't believe that I deserve to be a mother"*. For a short while, we took the edge off these distressing emotions.

We intentionally take time out to 'break' state. This enhances the integration and consolidation of the positive cognitive shifts. These well-chosen breaks provide a great way of connecting to the here and now. Tam and I both feel that this whole process is particularly healing and centring.

After a relaxing lunch break, a considerable amount of EFT tapping was done with both Di and Jim on their painful emotions and limiting beliefs until Di said she felt truly ready to welcome their baby and be a loving mother.

During the second morning Di and Jim enjoyed time alone. After lunch they took time out to prepare setup statements that related to exactly what they were wanting. I have included some of the setup phrases that we used.

* *Even though Jim was ok with what had happened and I wasn't until now, we deeply and completely respect one another's individual needs.*
* *Even though we don't consciously know how conception happens, we now both totally believe in our body's ability to bond my egg and Jim's sperm perfectly together because we are at one in our love.*
* *Even though we have waited for many years, we are now experiencing positive expectancy, happy in the knowledge we can be welcoming this baby into our lives with so much love.*

Reminder phrases: *Receiving this love into our lives. Allowing our bond of love to conceive this little one*

On our third day, Di and Jim wanted support and guidance to follow up and strengthen what they had already done with some positive imagery, using their words and making connections to their already great feelings. I have found that when clients use their own words to

172

plan and dream their dreams, they really connect to their inner wisdom and their vital force flows freely. Di wanted to enjoy her feelings as well as to picture her body healing completely and her ovary brimming full of energy and vitality and ovulating naturally. Whilst Di did this Jim gently tapped Di through the EFT sequence over and over again. There was tremendous energy, emotional excitement and joy flowing after this magical tapping procedure. They both reported their positive imagery and liberating feelings as we took time for a break together.

After our lunch break I asked them if they felt it would be helpful to build on this imagery and the good feelings as well as tapping along the way. They were both very enthusiastic about continuing this whilst they were in this wonderful state of flow. I took Jim and Di through an imaginary experience of truly loving oneness, with beautiful synchronised orgasms thrilling their body, mind and spirits. As they enjoyed the afterglow of imagined love in action, I continued to guide them through their perception of the joy of conception and a strong healthy egg softly and comfortably embedding safely in exactly the right place for their baby to grow. During the time of their beautiful experience, I added suggestions of continued benefits from their earlier EFT tapping routine, and of continuing to do this on their return home.

We discussed the power of their dreams, connecting to feelings and having a positive focus. They were both very happy to take home the CD recordings which we had made for them. These audios included what they were wanting, their dream journeys and positive tapping along the way. We heard two months after their visit that their healing and uplifting journey continues to be a support and inspiration to them both.

Trauma can create distorted writing on the walls of our minds. We are truly blessed now that we have EFT which erases these misperceptions which limit our lives. Tapping also has the potential of reconnecting to our birthright and life enhancing perceptions.

This was succinctly put by Bruce Lipton[3], (a cellular microbiologist and Stanford researcher) when he taught that our perception of life informs our biology. How our cells respond to life is based on what we believe. 'Perceptions' lie between the environment and cell expression.

If our perceptions are accurate, the resulting behaviour will be life enhancing. If we operate from misperceptions', our behaviour will be inappropriate and will jeopardize our vitality by compromising our health.

Part 5: Reconnecting to freedom in breathing

Case Study 3: Jamie

Jamie visited me last summer with streaming itchy eyes and other typical hay fever symptoms. Summertime for Jamie had been really miserable for the past twenty years. He had received little benefit from anti-histamine medication and he was finding his symptoms were getting progressively worse. This seems to occur mainly due to the fact that with practise we get better at doing most things. An example of this is riding a bike—with repetition we become more adept at cycling. Unfortunately, because of this, reactions or patterns of behaviour that we do not want—or which no longer serve a useful purpose can become habitual and we become 'better' at performing them.

Fortunately we can make traumas and limiting beliefs vanish as if by magic when using EFT to neutralise the emotional roots. I asked Jamie a few questions about his symptoms and also asked him what was happening around him at the time that he first noticed them. He said his first recollection of feeling tightness in his breath was when he was six years old, during an extended family camping holiday on a farm. Towards the end of this family holiday, his breathing became so difficult that his parents rushed him to the local village doctor. The doctor listened to his chest and sent him on his way with a prescription for anti-histamines. Every summer since that time, Jamie had been on anti-histamine medication.

During our first consultation, as we delved deeper into Jamie's memory of that breathless panic attack, he realised that it had happened well into the second week of the holiday. Throughout the whole of their time on the farm, the combine harvester was working in nearby fields.

Despite this, Jamie's 'allergic' reaction only appeared later on into the holiday. I asked him if he was enjoying his holiday before his breathing problem showed up. He recalled the holiday as being an absolutely great time because there were lots of cousins and friends to play with. Jamie said he had celebrated his sixth birthday around a week before he experienced his breathing trauma.

I became aware, as he talked about his memories, that he was experiencing some distressing symptoms. So, straight away, I asked him to follow me through the EFT routine. This period of tapping focused upon his current presenting symptoms and also connected him to the holiday experience. Open ended questions such as *"My hay fever symptoms happened because ...."* were also used. After a considerable amount of tapping Jamie had noticed a slight reduction in his discomfort. Throughout this session we made an audio CD to jog his memory of the EFT routine. This recording also included suggestions of homework. This homework was aimed at him using EFT with more specific descriptions of any discomfort he was feeling. I highlighted the tremendous value to him of really noticing any changes in the quality or level of symptoms occurring. Jamie was happy with the idea of chasing these symptoms especially after discussing the concept the of chasing the pain technique. Just before he left, he also wrote down some setup statements to work with such as:

* *Even though it was a great holiday with all my family— it just hasn't been fun having this reaction which is still bothering me right now.*
* *Even though I don't understand why I got this reaction part way through my holiday—I'm open to the possibility of discovering why, somehow.*

In addition to doing this tapping homework, I also asked him to ask his parents if they could throw any light on any earlier sensitising events to help us open other possible doors to his freedom.

On Jamie's return a week later he reported short bursts of improvements but then his symptoms quickly returned. Unfortunately, no one in the family had been able to shed any light on the problem at all. In our second session, we explored doing the EFT tapping procedure and Jamie just guessing at what might have happened on this fateful holiday. Whilst he talked about imagined events and feelings, he did the EFT tapping as if he was telling his story. Following this, there appeared to be some improvement in his symptoms. When I asked him what these symptoms reminded him of when he was younger, he looked blank. As his guessing had so far been fruitful, he was happy to tap and at the same time to make up imagined memories of what it reminded him of. There was no way of telling if his guesses were close to the truth or not. However, after this he reported a measurable improvement in the comfort of his throat and eyes which appeared to point to the possibility of his unconscious guesses being close to the truth or not. However, after this he reported a measurable improvement in the comfort of his throat and eyes which appeared to point to the possibility of his unconscious guesses being close to the truth.

Towards the end of this second session asked him if he could tell me the story of holiday again and do the EFT tapping as he did so. I recommended that he begin at the very start of the holiday describing just how he felt at the beginning of this holiday. He described his feelings of total and complete summer freedom and happiness. He had been involved in turning the hay as it dried in the sunshine. His family and friends had spent many hours during the first week living outside and picnicking in the fields. It occurred to me that as he talked in this very animated way, his breathing and eyes looked much clearer. It seemed as if he was re-living this freedom as he spoke—I asked him how much he wanted to live, breath and feel these easy feelings every summer from now on. Jamie did not need to answer my question; his enthusiastic nodding and energetic happy tapping answered that for me. On Jamie's third visit he reported a vast improvement in his hay fever symptoms. He also said that normally he would have tended to keep out of the garden and especially avoid times when he knew that his son was mowing the lawn. Instead, he chose to test the benefit of the tapping homework that he had done. Despite facing potentially difficult situations, no undue discomfort had occurred. I asked him if he was willing to go through telling his holiday story right from this lovely summer freedom experience to his difficulty in breath-ins, as well as visiting the doctor. I urged him to let me know if he experienced any emotional discomfort whilst he was doing this so that we could really use EFT to hone into some important issues.

As before, in telling his story he was very animated, telling how he was enjoying being involved in the haymaking and baling process. He said some of the older cousins made hay houses out of the bales and they all played in these tiny houses. At this point of the story his breathing became much more laboured so I tapped on him at the same time as he was tapping on himself. Later, when he calmed and we progressed through his story—stopping and clearing as we went—it became evident that one of the bales of hay had fallen on him creating a considerable amount of dust and fragments of straw which obviously hampered his breathing and frightened him.

Towards the end of the third session together, Jamie re-told his story without any undue disruption in his energy system. We completed our session with Jamie once again talking about the very beginning of his holiday. He described his total summer freedom and at the same time tapped himself continuously. At the peak of his joyful freedom experience, we created a positive kinesthetic anchor for those wonderful images and feelings. The following week I was thrilled when he rang to say that he wouldn't need another appointment because he still felt exactly the same freedom of mind and body that he remembered feeling before the hay bale incident.

Jamie also told me something else which fascinated me and is another interesting twist to his story. When he related his hay bale story to his Mother and was telling her about what had happened on that holiday, she looked really shocked. Then, she immediately told Jamie her story. Apparently, when he was only two days old, they had had to call an ambulance to take him to hospital because he was fighting for his breath. When they arrived at the accident and emergency department the doctor there used a special tube to clear a blockage of mucous from his mouth and throat.

Jamie wisely tapped on himself as his mother recounted this trauma to him. His mother said, at the time she was sure that her little two day old baby was going to die. She said Jamie had turned blue and the only thing she could think to do whilst she waited for help was to rub his back whilst he lay with his head hanging down over her knees. Her distress at her powerlessness and the emotional charge within her in telling her story was very obvious to Jamie so he asked his dear mother to just follow him through the tapping routine as she talked.

Co-incidence maybe—I think not. I believe this frightening experience whilst playing in the hay, reminded his unconscious of nearly dying as a two day old newborn baby. At six years old, once again his unconscious mind was understandably triggered by the hay bale falling and his difficulty in breathing. This created an extreme reaction and association to the powerlessness that he felt as a little baby fighting for his breath and the six year old's difficulty in breathing.

I had a Christmas card from Jamie last Christmas, also signed by his mother, in which they said how much happier they both felt after neutralising this extremely fearful memory from the archives of their minds.

References:

Hogan, Kevin, 'Through The Open Door—Secrets of Self-Hypnosis', (Pelican, 2000) (chapter 16 was my earliest reported interventions for my own eyesight improvements)

O'Connor, Joseph 8c Seymour, John, 'Introducing Neuro-Linguistic Programming— The New Psychology of Personal Excellence', (Aquarian Press, 1990)

Lipton, Bruce, 'The Biology of Belief, (Hay House, 2008)

Appendix Two

This is an extract from Gary Craig's book "Meet the Unseen Therapist"

Mary Llewellyn has received Gary Craig's permission to share pages from his book "The Unseen Therapist" in "EFT constellations" heart-centred processes for self-confidence and healthy independence. These pages are available for you to read in the appendix of this book.

Meet the Unseen Therapist
(In whom the impossible becomes routine)

The Unseen Therapist is your "spiritual healer within."

She is ever-present and, when you learn to use Her skills properly, you will find She is vastly more powerful than drugs surgeries and other man-made attempts at healing. She represents a healing revolution that leaves your current beliefs behind and whisks you off on a magic carpet ride into your personal healing cosmos.

This is where the impossible becomes routine. It is where your ultimate remedy resides and, once mastered, it is also where your view of the entire healing field will shift. Your need for drugs and surgeries will be minimized or erased. Side effects will fade into near nothingness and heavy expenses will be dramatically curtailed. In their place will emerge creative possibilities that will bring new levels of healing into your hands.

If you are a patient, you can draw on The Unseen Therapist for self-help. If you are a doctor, nurse, therapist or other practitioner, you can use Her abundant support before resorting to invasive procedures and their side-effects.

To do Her work She needs only your readiness and proper invitation.

Within these pages, you will learn how to develop that readiness and provide that invitation. Doing so involves a very doable process that can generate impressive benefits even while you are learning. You may go as far as you wish and are limited only by your motivation.

Once mastered to the ultimate degree, you will hold the equivalent of a magic wand that delivers benefits for every ailment imaginable. This includes everything from a common headache - to every conceivable emotional issue - to the apparently hopeless diseases for which conventional methods often fail.

The Unseen Therapist lives within each of us — no exceptions — and thus is readily available to you. A child can call on Her and get impressive results. So can a prisoner, housewife, war veteran or doctor. It doesn't matter about your educational level either. You only need to be able to read this book. Nor does it matter whether you are rich or poor, young or old, male or female, athletic or crippled. She is waiting — and eager — to bring healing well beyond your expectations'

She is the loving essence of all spiritual practices and thus does not conflict with anyone's Divine preferences. She is known by many names, including: Love, God, Source, Peace, Jesus, Buddha, Yahweh, Muhammad, Allah, Higher Intelligence, Spirit, Holy Spirit, Jehovah, Guidance, Inner Wisdom, Ruach Hakodesh and more. I've had clients who prefer to call Her Nature or the Ocean Waves. Others equate Her with the loving memory of a grandmother, a pet or a coach. It doesn't matter which name you give Her as She has no ego.

Further, She is not actually a "she" because She has no body and thus no gender. I refer to Her as a She because females are generally considered to be softer and more compassionate than males. But, if you prefer, you can call Her a He — or an It — or even a Cloud or a Breeze. Your choice. What you call Her doesn't change who She is.

I am bringing you this advancement as an outsider to the healing profession. I am a Stanford trained engineer with no formal education in medicine, therapy or the like. As a result, I am free to innovate because I am not burdened by the hand-me-down beliefs that permeate the healing professions. While medicine has certainly provided some impressive innovations, those advances are small when compared to your possibilities that come from within.

Engineers prefer to simplify. We look at a complex process, break it down into essential pieces, throw out the unnecessary parts and then rebuild it into a streamlined procedure. The results, in this case, is The Unseen Therapist and Her one natural remedy for everything.

"But Gary," you might ask, "haven't people been using similar methods — like prayer and distance healing — for many years?"

Yes, of course, and it was those stunning results that helped point me in this direction. What I have added, however, is a companion healing process (The Personal Peace Procedure) that brings unique focus to your issue(s). This focus adds more power to your healing prayers and allows them to be answered with greater reliability, depth and efficiency.

That's why The Unseen Therapist, together with our companion process, is already reshaping our healing landscape. This is easily verified in "A Peek at Your Possibilities" (later in this book) which includes dramatic examples of this combo at work. These samples range from a stroke recovery, to the fear of dogs, to disappearing blood clots, to hospital miracles and beyond.

This is a practical book that displays how to gain these benefits without the debatable theologies as to why. Thus, you will be connecting with the vast healing power of your spiritual essence while avoiding theological speculation. This allows you to see beyond conventional methods so that the true cause of your ailments is revealed.

And that cause is of the mind. It is emotional, not physical.

This simplifies the entire health field and allows you to step onto a bridge that leads to an ultimate remedy with healing benefits unimagined by man-made therapies. New doors, new vistas and impressive benefits await you.

Appendix Three

MY PERSONAL
TRANSFORMATIONAL STORY

I was brought up within a very strict religious sect. I felt powerless and I couldn't break free. As I woke up to the life I was living at many times, I felt distress and separation. There were so many things I really wanted to do but I had no choice. The children in my class thought I was strange and all I wanted was to belong. When they asked me to play after school, I had to say "No". I wished I could tell them why. I could not explain because no one had told me why I was not allowed to play.

I was the youngest of six children. I was born into a really loving family who belong to the Exclusive Brethren, a strict religious sect. Three of my elder brothers left the sect and our family home. I was young when this happened and nobody told me where my brothers had gone nor why. I felt sad, confused and I did miss them. I thought my parents were sad even though nobody talked about it. I wished I could make a difference but I didn't know how to change what was happening. My parents had been born into this sect and they honestly believed this was their true calling.

As I grew older I realised that my parents would never leave the sect. In the future if I married I discovered that it would have to be to a member of the sect. Any other choice would have meant I risked total separation from my beautiful family as well as the sect. After marrying a member of the sect I had to leave home and live near to my husband's work and his family. I missed the closeness of my own family and I searched for love and connection, which is very important to me. When I was married I could not work. My place was in the home and I was expected to be subservient to my husband.

Years later, when our eldest daughter reached school age I knew I absolutely could not bring up my children within that sect. Fortunately, my husband and I felt the same way about this. Neither of us wanted our lovely daughters to live their lives like that. If we left the sect, there had to be complete separation from my parents as well as from my remaining brother and sister who still belonged to the sect. Taking this step was an unbelievable wrench. In spite of this I was certain that what we had to do was right for our daughters, my husband as well as for me. Up until that time in my life I had been passive.

My husband and I prepared to leave this sect. The huge decision we were about to make meant that I could not have any contact with my mum, dad, sister or brother. Now we were on our own - a young family bound together with love and a positive intention for all of our lives. At last my husband our children and I were able to meet people from all walks of life. We were free to make our own choices. Going to work was then a possibility if I wanted to. Shortly after leaving my family and the organisation, we welcomed into our lives the birth of our beautiful third daughter in 1970.

Five years later in 1975 with another baby on the way, I discovered that the National Childbirth Trust (NCT) was recommending a new birthing book by Erna Wright. This book fascinated me so much so that before the birth of our youngest daughter I learnt to practise what I now know to be self-hypnosis. My intention in doing this was to use hypnosis throughout her birth. The joy I felt during her birth was a natural and magical experience and it mobilized me into wanting to learn more about the mind-body relationship. Early each day I studied before my husband and children woke up. I was so happy as well as hungry to learn and it was a real gift to have this possibility in my life now. I just knew within every fibre of my being that I was going to help people to be more positive and also to benefit from using self-hypnosis in their lives.

When I traced my two eldest brothers who had left home it was so lovely to be in touch, they knew and understood exactly how I felt. They left the sect and since then they had been free to live their lives. For a long time I also searched for my third eldest brother David. When I failed to find him I got in touch with the Salvation Army and asked them if they could trace him for me. After six months they contacted me to say they had found him and that he may be in touch with me. When he rang a short while later I was so excited, it was unbelievably beautiful to hear his voice again. It was as if the last 19 years of separation had melted away. Then, he told me that he had been a practising hypnotherapist for 17 years and was passionate about it. I couldn't believe it, how had he and I both been attracted to hypnosis? Any interest in hypnosis would have been a dark and impossible profession to explore before separating from the sect.

It was very obvious to me that my brother was just as passionate as I was about helping others to be happy and free. As we talked over old childhood times together we both recalled our dear dad often arriving home from his work with tears of joy in his eyes. This would always be because, as an herbalist he was able to help someone to feel better. We then guessed that our Dad's desire to help others to heal with his herbs in the 1950's was the thread of love and compassion running though all of our lives.

As there was little clinical hypnosis being taught or used in the early 70's it seemed instinctively right at that time for my brother David to be my teacher and supervisor. After studying with him and continuing my psychology training I couldn't wait to share the benefits to be gained from teaching others self-hypnosis. In 1980 I began my private practise as a hypnotherapist and from that moment, I knew that I was on the path that I was meant to be on. This was my calling and today thirty-six years later I absolutely love working with clients. I am so happy for them, too, when they ring to say they don't need their next appointment.

My aim then, and it is exactly the same now; I want people not to need me. My passion for freedom for my children, my clients and myself opened the way to my learning EFT. Whilst using these techniques myself and exploring them with my clients I discovered that hypnosis and EFT could be combined into an intuitive bridge. This process facilitates a re-connection to who we really are. We can freely receive and enjoy the way we were born to be. We are all as we were intended to be whatever has happened in our lives. The gifts we were given when we were born may have been wrapped up for a while and now we can open our hearts and welcome them into our lives where they truly belong.

Acknowledgements

After learning and teaching Emotional Freedom Techniques (EFT), I noticed positive changes happening in clients, students and in my life too. I felt deeply passionate and determined to spread this further by writing this book.

This acknowledgement section of my book is a challenge - there are those that I would dearly love to mention many who have supported me over the years and made so much possible for me. At this time, I am holding those in my thoughts who are specifically connected to this book. Without my husband Tam's help this would never have been written. He has consistently supported me emotionally and especially technically.

I have learnt and received priceless gifts from all of you who have so generously shared your development of energy therapies. Thank you dear Gary Craig, Tapas Fleming, Dr Larry Nims and Donna Eden.

To all of my clients, students and supervisees, thank you for being my ongoing teachers. I learnt so much from you often without realising it at the time. Then later on reflection, I know without you all, this book would never have been written. Your determination and trust in our work together was heart-warming and deeply touching.

My loving parents, brothers and sister understood intuitively our mind, body, heart and soul healing. They taught me about trusting with love in my life. I have been completely and delightfully blessed with four very loving daughters as well as grandchildren who bring so much joy.

Sasha Allenby believed, supported and inspired me throughout the writing of this book. She willing gave love, laughter and a guiding light to my writing. Thank you Sasha too for creating the "Author Master Mind Group" This group was inspirational it incorporated every one of us. This meant we all received your consistent encouragement and the delight of us all being in this life changing experience together. I know I have learnt so much from you, bless you with love sweet heart.

Lois Rose with your help, support and easy style, I found I could relax and totally trust you. I immediately knew I was held in very confident and gifted hands. As soon as you talked about editing for me I felt truly thankful, so much lighter and very happy. Thank you lovely Lois.

RESOURCES

Useful Resources and References when working with Children

Carrington, Dr Patricia PhD. (2008) A Guide to TappyBear Pace Educational Systems, Inc USA *This is a beautiful book which is helpful for children as well as adults. However it appears to be no longer in print. It may be possible to get hold of a used copy.*

Hudson, Linda (2009) Scrips & Strategies in Hypnotherapy with Children – Crown House Publishing **www.crownhousepublishing.com**

Wiese, Jo with Wells, Steve (2004) Rose and the Night Monsters Watford Publishing Aus *This book sits on our waiting room table for children to pick up and read. The pictures and the story is pitched beautifully to captureae little ones imagination as well as help them in their lives.*

Wood, Linda – **Magic Button Bears for children and adults**.
Visits her website to find her latest up to date details. For many years she has bought and adapted bears and given them tapping points these are very individual over the years I have bought a variety of Linda's bears for clients and grandchildren. www.tappingtoheal.com

Yates, Brad (2010) The Wizards Wish - www.bradyates.net

Here is another book that is well loved by parents and their children when they come to visit us.

This list would not be complete without introducing TAPPY BEAR and other toys which are available for children who visit. This friendly faced bear can be hugged cuddled and also tapped on this is because TAPPY BEAR is well equipped with little buttons which can locate where they can tap this loveable bear and to also learn when the points are on their own little bodies too. However as we are never too old to hug a cuddly bear I have found many older clients enjoy talking too and tapping TEDDY whilst sharing their emotions.

Since compiling this list to support children unfortunately Tappybear is no longer for sale however there are bears which are special created by Linda Wood details above.

Various Therapies

Be Set Free Fast (BSFF)

BSFF is a highly focused Energy Therapy method for eliminating the emotional roots and self-limiting belief systems that are embedded in the subconscious mind, and which automatically determine and control most of our experience, self-expression and behaviour. These unresolved negative emotions and beliefs create and maintain psychological and physical symptoms, which automatically result in mental, emotional, physical, energetic spiritual and life adjustment problems, including many medical, and health problems. BSFF eliminates these subconscious programs quickly and gently. BE SET FREE FAST^{SM} is a descriptive acronym for "Behavioural & Emotional Symptom Elimination Training For Resolving Excess Emotion: Fear, Anger, Sadness & Trauma."

For more information and products on Dr Larry Nims the developer of BSFF visit his website :-www.BeSetFreeFast.com

Emotional Freedom Techniques

EFT is a powerful relatively new discovery that combines two well established sciences so you can benefit from both at the same time:

1. Mind Body Medicine
2. Acupuncture (without needles).

In essence, EFT is an emotional version of acupuncture wherein we stimulate certain meridian points by tapping on them with our fingertips. This addresses a new cause for emotional issues (unbalanced energy meridians). Properly done, this frequently reduces the therapeutic process from months or years down to hours or minutes. And, since emotional stress can contribute to pain, disease and physical ailments, we often find that EFT provides astonishing physical relief.

For more information visit the website at: www.emofree.com

Simple Energy Techniques (SET)

SET is a collection of simple and user-friendly energy techniques, which can provide significant relief for a wide range of emotional problems, and some physical problems. Although the techniques are simple to use, the results of using them can be quite profound.

For more information visit the website at:-

http://www.eftdownunder.com/SET.html

Tapas Accupuncture Technique (TAT)

TAT is an easy way to dissolve stress, limiting beliefs, and negativity. You can use TAT to get over stuff without judgment, analysis, or reliving anything. The process is a combination of the TAT Pose (touching acupressure points on the face and back of the head) while putting attention on the Steps of TAT (a set of freeing and empowering intentions). It was developed by Tapas Fleming.

You can download details of the steps from her site or buy DVD's to increase your understanding of the technique and can be obtained from Tapas Flemings site :-

www.unstressforsuccess.com

Life Inventory course – this website offers you free material to explore your own values and purpose in life. The website is listed for you to visit.

http://www.lifevaluesinventory.org

CD Resources Created Personally For Individual Clients

Hypnotherapy and also Journal Support CDs

Mary Llewellyn - Creates individually recorded CDs for her clients to use for Mind Body Healing as well as for support through their journal writing.

For details visit her website :-

www.TickhillClinic.com or email Mary Llewellyn at:- MairLLLL@ aol.com

PROFESSIONAL EQUIPMENT

Bio Feedback Monitor

This machine provides insight into how our thoughts affect our physiology. Even hidden emotions reveal themselves whilst using this on yourself or others. It is helpful for our understanding as well as offering clearer guidance for clients. I use it in the corporate, sports and personal development work that I do with adults as well as children.

Available from Website: Hypno-quip.co.uk

G.S.R Galvanic Skin Response monitor.

This is another name for the bio feedback monitor described earlier.

Hypnocom

Readers who are also hypnotherapists or relaxation therapy practitioners benefit from using this machine to record CDs for their clients meditation or hypnotherapy. It is simple to use and allows you to incorporate background music or natural sounds together with your voice to guide others through a relaxation or hypnotic process which they can use at home. This strengthens, supports and benefits their therapy time with you. It can also be used last thing at night to help with sleep. Many say that it inspires confidence. Other clients notice it supports them and allows them to let go of unhelpful emotions. Available from Website: Hypno-quip.co.uk

MEDITATION AND YOGA PRACTISE WEBSITE – www. yogaglow.com search for David Harshada Wagner *This site and David together with other practitioners offers guided meditation and yoga. Subscribing to this website enables you to pay a modest monthly fee for regular sessions of the therapies offered.*

About the Author

Author – EFT Founding Master Mary Llewellyn

From 1980 Mary practiced hypnosis with clients who came to her clinic. While they were in their hypnotic state, she noticed that some spontaneously reconnected to their innate resources. After training in EFT Mary found that this reconnection could be brought about by linking EFT with hypnosis; Mary observes herself and others and, using what she sees, she moves towards and investigates ways to love better. Mary absolutely loves it when clients cancel and say, "What we did together worked wonders." Her intention has always been to empower others. She wrote this book for that reason.

Qualifications:

BA(Hons) Psychology.
Post Graduate Advanced Diploma. in Child Development
Hypnotherapy Practitioner Diploma GHSC. Dip
EFT Master Practitioner Certificate & Trainer
EFT Honors Level Certificate
BSFF Practitioner & Trainer
TAT Practitioner

Professional Membership:

The British Psychological Society
The National Council of Psychotherapists

The National Council for Hypnotherapists.
The Assn for the Advancement of Meridian Therapy Techniques.
The General Hypnotherapy Register.
The EFT Universe

Professional Fellowships:

The Royal Society of Arts.
The Hypnotherapy Research Society.

Mary is a psychotherapist/hypnotherapist and energy therapist she works full-time at The Tickhill Clinic. This is a complementary therapy centre in the heart of a South Yorkshire village in the UK. She holds an honours degree in psychology and post graduate training in psychotherapy. She has worked in adult, family as well as child care programmes. She is a therapist with over 34 years of experience in full time private practice.

Mary is an eclectic therapist using a comprehensive approach to healing, this involves integrating traditional with newer, complementary models of energy psychology. Mary has been awarded an EFT Master Practitioner and Academic Certificate Honors Level status by Gary Craig the developer of EFT.

Mary utilises specialized techniques in the treatment of PTSD, depression, anxiety and phobias. Her work with addictions involves eating disorders as well as drug and alcohol abuse. Mary is as comfortable working within the corporate world as the sports arena. Within the corporate world she helps professionals develop skills with people, anger management and assertive behaviour training. She says she feels truly honoured to be invited into so many aspects of her clients lives.

Mary is an accredited trainer with the National Council of Psychotherapy, The Association for the Advancement of Meridian Therapy Techniques, The National Council of Hypnotherapy, The EFT Universe as well as Be Set Free Fast (BSFF). In the last 19 years Mary has trained therapists and trainers Worldwide in Energy Psychology Techniques.

Many is an accredited supervisor with the National Council of Psychotherapy, The Association for the Advancement of Meridian Therapy Techniques, The National Council of Hypnotherapy, The Hypnotherapy Research Society and The General Hypnotherapy Register.

Printed in the United States
By Bookmasters